in my
FOOTSTEPS
a Cape Cod travel guide

CHRISTOPHER SETTERLUND

Schiffer Publishing Ltd

4880 Lower Valley Road • Atglen, PA 19310

Library of Congress Control Number: 2013942061

Designed by John P. Cheek
Cover design by Justin Watkinson
Type set in Helvetica Neue

ISBN: 978-0-7643-4209-7
Printed in China

Published by Schiffer Publishing, Ltd.
4880 Lower Valley Road
Atglen, PA 19310
Phone: (610) 593-1777; Fax: (610) 593-2002
E-mail: Info@schifferbooks.com

For our complete selection of fine books on this and related subjects, please visit our website at **www.schifferbooks.com**. You may also write for a free catalog.

This book may be purchased from the publisher. Please try your bookstore first.

We are always looking for people to write books on new and related subjects. If you have an idea for a book, please contact us at **proposals@schifferbooks.com**

Schiffer Publishing's titles are available at special discounts for bulk purchases for sales promotions or premiums. Special editions, including personalized covers, corporate imprints, and excerpts can be created in large quantities for special needs. For more information, contact the publisher.

CONTENTS

VIII. Wellfleet

IX. Truro

X. Provincetown

XI. Chatham

XII. Harwich

XIII. West Dennis & South Dennis

XIV. Yarmouth

INTRODUCTION

For most visitors, Cape Cod probably brings to mind some common themes: beaches, clam chowder, and whale watches, to name a few. This is what most people think of when they think of Cape Cod and usually is what their visiting experience encompasses.

For me, Cape Cod is in my blood; it is my family. I am a twelfth generation Cape Codder with my lineage dating back to the 17th century. The most well known names in Cape Cod history: Doane, Nickerson, Wixon, Chase, and Crowell are sprinkled throughout my family tree. I have been to every nook and cranny of this great area and want to share with you some places you know and many that you may not. These places, their stories, their history, are what make Cape Cod such a unique place to live and visit.

This travel guide is designed to make visiting Cape Cod as convenient as possible. The sites to see are all in geographical order as one would see them, beginning with the trip over the Sagamore Bridge. This approach will help any visitor see as many beautiful spots on the Cape while conserving time and gas. Have fun and happy traveling!

A VIEW OF THE SAGAMORE BRIDGE FROM THE MAINLAND SIDE OF THE CAPE COD CANAL.

Note: At the time of publication, all fees and regulations were accurate. They are subject to change.

I

SANDWICH

GPS: (41.772272,-70.492512)
Directions: Cross over the Sagamore Bridge on Rt. 6 and take Exit 1C. At the end of the exit ramp, turn right onto Sandwich Road which becomes Route 6A. Follow it 2.6 miles, then turn left at the stop light onto Tupper Road. Take the first right onto Town Neck Road, and follow it 0.6 miles to the first destination. (Distance: 4.5 mi. Driving time from the bridge: 10 mins.)

1. Eastern Mouth of the Cape Cod Canal

The eastern mouth of the Cape Cod Canal is reached by taking a drive down Town Neck Road to Town Neck Beach. There is a very rocky beach between the parking area and the breakwater of the Canal. The waves pull at the rocks creating a crackling sound that can be hypnotic at times. From the breakwater, one can see straight across to Scusset Beach in Sagamore. It is often possible to see vessels, both large and small, pass by this spot as they go through the

A SHIP EXITING THE EASTERN MOUTH OF THE CAPE COD CANAL.

Canal and head out into Cape Cod Bay. At a maximum width of 540 feet, the Canal carries over 20,000 ships through its waters annually. It was opened on a limited basis in 1914 and finished in 1916, although the idea of a canal in the area was originally pondered by Miles Standish as early as 1623. Since the Canal was not around a hundred years ago, towns, like Wareham, on the northern shore of the Canal consider themselves to be a part of the Cape.

A trail leads from the eastern end of the Canal at the bay to the *Sandwich Marina*. This is an active place used by pleasure craft, fishermen, lobstermen, and the U.S. Coast Guard, whose station is nearby. The Cape Cod Canal Visitor Center is also here, at 60 Ed Moffitt Drive. It is run by the Army Corps of Engineers. On the other side of the marina is a power plant, owned and run by the Atlanta-based energy company, Mirant. This is the perfect place to begin a walk, run, or bike ride along the Canal.

Important Info
- Daily parking: $10
- No lifeguard or concessions
- Dogs allowed Labor Day-Memorial Day

GPS: (41.764174,-70.485946)

Directions from Previous Site: From Town Neck Beach return to Tupper Avenue, turn left, the turn left again onto Rt. 6A at the traffic light. Follow it 0.4 miles to the next traffic light and turn left onto Jarves Street. Take the 2ᵈ left onto Church Street then the 1ˢᵗ right onto Harbor Street. Continue onto Boardwalk Road and to the parking area for the Boardwalk, your next destination. (Distance: 1.9 mi. Driving time: 8 mins.)

2. Boardwalk Beach

Boardwalk Beach is a little difficult for the novice to find; the only sign for the boardwalk is a thin white pole on Jarves Street just off of Rt. 6A, with "Boardwalk" and an arrow pointing you in the right direction.

Once you have found it, however, this spot is incredible; nearly all of the boards that make up the walkway are adorned with messages. From memories of 9/11 to good wishes for America, from local business names to couples celebrating their love, the boardwalk in Sandwich is less of a way to reach the beach than of a slice of American life. It is tempting to stop and read each of the messages adorning the 1,000 feet of boards that carry you across the marsh.

As you follow the boardwalk, you will have some tremendous views of the natural life in the surrounding salt marsh ecosystem. The view of the actual beach is astounding as well. The boardwalk leads you up a dune where you can see the nearby Cape Cod Canal and across the water to Sagamore Beach and Plymouth. Visitors can walk the boardwalk, reading the messages on each plank, then relax on a beautiful beach with a great view.

Important Info
- Daily parking $10
- No lifeguard or concessions
- Dogs allowed Labor Day-Memorial Day

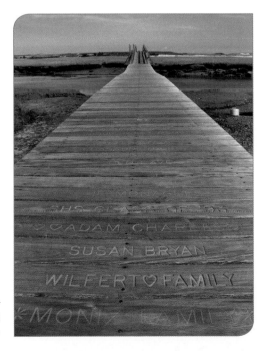

THE BOARDWALK AT BOARDWALK BEACH IN SANDWICH.

Town Neck Beach & Boardwalk Beach
Sandwich

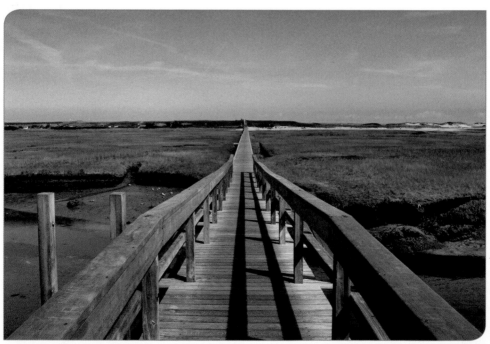

THE BOARDWALK AT BOARDWALK BEACH IN SANDWICH.

3. Shawme-Crowell State Forest

Shawme-Crowell State Forest gets its name from the Native Americans, who called the area around Sandwich "Shawme."It can be entered from two directions: trails will be found across the street from the *Heritage Museum & Gardens* off Grove Street, or you can use the main entrance on Rt. 130.

The forest offers a great hike through over 700 acres of forest. It has a year-round campground with 285 sites available and is filled with lots of picnic areas providing tremendous views of the pine forest.

The trails leading from Grove Street have clever names such as the Coyote Den, Raccoon Den, Sherris Berries, and Mayflower trails. They parallel the highway at spots so it is difficult to get lost.

The main entrance features roads with letter names, Road A for example, which make them easy to follow. There is a playground for the children on Road C next to the Friends Pavilion, deep inside the forest, which can be used for larger gatherings. There are more than fifteen miles of roads and trails to be walked. Often, visitors will see horseback riders going from one old dirt fire road to another. It is easy to spend an entire day wandering Shawme-Crowell State Forest, even if you are not camping out.

Important Info
- Free entrance
- Camping: resident $12; non-resident $15 per night

THE FRIENDS PAVILION.

THE MAIN ROAD INTO SHAWME-CROWELL STATE FOREST.

GPS: (41.749175,-70.508378)

Directions from Previous Site: When leaving Shawme-Crowell State Forest, turn right onto Main Street (Rt. 130). Follow it 0.6 miles, then turn right onto Pine Street. Follow it 0.6 miles, where Grove Street intersects Pine Street. You will see the main gate and parking on the left. (Distance: 1.2 mi. Driving Time: 3 mins.)

4. Heritage Museum & Gardens

This is a perfect way to spend a day on Cape Cod. *Heritage Museum & Gardens* has so much to see and do.

The land was first settled in 1677 by Lydia Wing Hamilton Abbott. To this day the Wing family farm makes up part of the Heritage grounds.

Among the exhibits is the J.K. Lilly Automobile Museum, which is in a beautiful, round, Shaker stone barn and contains more than thirty classic vehicles. The more well known are a 1913 Ford Model T, Gary Cooper's Duesenberg, and President William H. Taft's parade vehicle. There is also an American History Museum and the Old East Windmill. The windmill was built in Orleans in

A GARDEN AT HERITAGE MUSEUM & GARDENS.

1800. It was sold to Heritage in 1968 and painstakingly moved thirty-two miles to its current location. There are often temporary exhibits in addition to the permanent collection.

The gardens here are spectacular, encompassing one hundred acres and including labeled trees and shrubs, specially designed gardens, and large lawns. These gardens are perfect in any season.

The Heritage Museum & Gardens are open May 1st to October 31st from 10 a.m. to 5 p.m.. It offers an amazing collection of American history and a beautiful natural environment that all visitors to Cape Cod should take the time to see.

Important Info:
• Admission: adults: $15; youth (3-12), $7

THE ENTRANCE TO HERITAGE MUSEUM & GARDENS.

J.K. LILLY AUTOMOBILE MUSEUM

GPS: (41.75523,-70.498206)

Directions from Previous Site: Coming out of the Heritage parking area, bear right on Grove Street and follow it 0.8 miles. Turn right onto Main Street, then bear right onto Water Street. Follow it 0.2 miles to the next destination on the right. (Distance: 1.1 mi. Driving Time: 3 mins.)

5. Sandwich Historic Center

Cape Cod has many historic places, and each town has a historic center. Sandwich, however, is the oldest town on the Cape, and its historic center should be the first one you visit. There is no shortage of parking places.

Hoxie House, on Water Street, is as good a place as any to begin a walk through town. The house dates to 1675 and was the home of the Reverend John Smith and his large family. This traditional "salt box" style house is the oldest of this type on Cape Cod. It was purchased by Capt. Abraham Hoxie in the mid-19th century, which is how it got its name. It is surprisingly one of few historic homes on the Cape in its original location, as so many have been moved to other locations in the attempt to preserve them. It is open for tours from June through September.

A few houses away is the Thornton W. Burgess Museum. Located in the Deacon Eldred House, built in 1756, this museum is dedicated to Burgess, an author and creator of such beloved children's book characters as Peter Rabbit. The museum is open from approximately Memorial Day to Columbus Day.

Continue walking past the Burgess Museum to see some panoramic views of Shawme Pond. On the edge of the pond is another historic site, Dexter's Grist Mill, which still operates today and offers freshly ground cornmeal for sale inside. The mill was built in 1654 and restored in 1961. Thomas Dexter, for whom it is named, began building grist mills on the site in 1637, to grind grain into flour and meal. The water turns the wooden wheel of the mill, then continues under the street.

There is a running spring next to the stone wall that borders the mill grounds. People come from all over to fill their water jugs with its fresh water.

As you walk around town, you will enjoy many historic, well maintained homes and businesses. It is a great place to park and take a leisurely walk through the oldest town on Cape Cod: Sandwich.

Important Info:
- Hoxie House/Dexter Grist Mill combo admission: adults, $5/children, $3
- Burgess Museum: admission by donation

HOXIE HOUSE

THORNTON BURGESS MUSEUM

DEXTER'S GRIST MILL

NEWCOMB TAVERN, SANDWICH

GPS: (41.738528,-70.381318)

Directions from Previous Site: Continue on Water Street then take the first left onto School Street. At Main Street turn right and continue to Rt. 6A. Make a slight right turn onto Rt. 6A and follow it 5.1 miles. Turn left onto Sandy Neck Road and follow it to the end. (Distance: 6.9 mi. Driving Time: 14 mins.)

6. Sandy Neck Beach & Sandy Neck Trails

Sandy Neck Beach is one of the most popular beaches on the Cape. The beach can be quite rocky closer to the water, but is so large that finding a comfortable spot is not difficult. The famed dunes of Sandy Neck have long been protected by locals. As far back as the 1700s, measures were put in place to keep the dunes from eroding. Farmers were told not to allow their herds to graze there and whaling ships anchored offshore were limited in the wood they could take from the Sandy Neck area for their boilers.

Located directly across from the ranger station on Sandy Neck Road is a sign for the Sandy Neck Nature Trails. There are six walking trails of varying distances, a horse trail, a beach access trail, and some connectors. Should you choose, you can walk more than six miles east, ending at a strip of seaside homes and the lighthouse, opposite Barnstable Harbor. Even if you don't go the full distance, the Sandy Neck Trails have some amazing natural beauty and a few pieces of history as well. You start out on the Beach Access Trail, which goes along the beach. With permits, this is open to off-road vehicles at certain times of the year. The Marsh Trail breaks off to the right and follows the border of the dunes and the salt marsh, moving east. The salt marsh is on the right, complete with several small birdhouses and an osprey nest situated on top of a pole out in the marsh.

Staying on the Marsh Trail, after Trail 1 breaks off to the left and heads to the Bay, you will start to see the larger dunes that Sandy Neck is known for, with even better views further along. Keep walking along the Marsh Trail and you will notice the first of many small cottages, most of them a hundred years old, that dot the land. These are great reminders of what Sandy Neck was like in the early 20th century, when it was part of the fishing and whaling industry. The cottages are usually occupied in the summer, so be respectful of their property.

For the most part, until you reach Trail 2 the land is uniform, mainly beach sand. The majestic dunes are in plain sight the entire time. However, once you pass Trail 2 and a small guard shack located just off of the trail, the land begins to change a bit. There are still mountainous dunes, but trees become more abundant, as do the fishing cottages. There is no Trail 3, so take Trails 2 or 4 for beach access. Trail 4 will lead you through the dunes and spotty trees and vegetation to the beach and offers a tremendous view.

Branching off of Trail 4 is a trail designated for horseback riding, but it is obviously fine for human use as well. This trail takes you winding through the trees, and, if not for the constant hum of the ocean waves, you might forget that a beach is close by. There are many tiny ponds scattered throughout this area, but swimming in them is probably not possible or recommended.

This area of Sandy Neck is also rich in wildlife. Many species of birds, including hawks and osprey, will fly by. On the ground, the most common animals spotted are squirrels, but raccoons, skunks, and an occasional deer can be seen as well.

As the Marsh Trail becomes Trail 5, it weaves its way through the trees and will take you out to the beach. It is here that you may go left and head back to the parking lot or continue onto Trail 6 and the tip of Sandy Neck. It is a long walk, but the views are incredible. The cottages, the marsh, the dunes, the trees, ponds, trails, and lighthouse all make for an amazing hike.

Important Info:

- Daily parking: $15
- Lifeguard and concessions in season
- ORV seasonal pass: Non-Resident: $160
- Dogs allowed Labor Day-Memorial Day

A COTTAGE ALONG THE SANDY NECK TRAILS.

THE FAMED DUNES AT SANDY NECK.

II

WEST BARNSTABLE
& CUMMAQUID

GPS: (41.700474,-70.298942)

Directions from Previous Site: Follow Sandy Neck Road back to Rt. 6A and turn left onto Rt. 6A. The Coast Guard Heritage Museum is 6.6 miles on the right. (Distance: 7.8 mi. Driving Time: 16 mins.)

1. Coast Guard Heritage Museum & Old Jail
West Barnstable

With the Coast Guard's connection to Cape Cod and its history, it is only natural that there is a Coast Guard Heritage Museum located here. It is at Cobb's Hill, opposite the Unitarian Church of West Barnstable. The museum opened in 2005 in a building was once a United States Customs House. Hours are 10 a.m. to 3 p.m., Tuesday to Saturday, from May through mid-October.

Located on the grounds of the Coast Guard Heritage Museum, another piece of Cape Cod and American history is known as "The Oldest Wooden Jail in America." The Old Jail is purported to have been built in the 1690s and was in use until a new stone jail was built around 1820.

The jail was situated on private property on Old Jail Lane, just west of the Coast Guard Heritage Museum, until 1972. The owner thought it was an old barn. Thankfully, she brought Barnstable Country Chief Deputy Sheriff Louis Cataldo to view the "barn." In 1949, Cataldo had founded Tales of Cape Cod, a repository of Cape history. When he realized what the barn really was, he made it a mission to save it and move it.

The Old Jail is opened Tuesdays, Thursdays, and Saturdays from May through mid-November. It is a hidden gem of Cape history. After walking through the Old Jail a drive down the narrow, secluded, Old Jail Lane is recommended as well. It is a perfect capper to the experience.

Important Info:
- Coast Guard Museum: Admission $5/children under 10 are free
- Old Jail: Free admission – donations welcome

COAST GUARD HERITAGE MUSEUM

THE OLD JAIL

GPS: (41.708972,-70.27672)

Directions from Previous Site: Coming out of the Coast Guard Heritage Museum, turn right onto Rt. 6A and follow it 1.4 miles. Turn left onto Bone Hill Road, follow it 0.2 miles. Look for a white Sanctuary sign on the left and follow the driveway to the Visitor Center parking area. (Distance: 1.5 mi. Driving Time: 3 mins.)

2. Long Pasture Wildlife Sanctuary
Cummaquid

This 110-acre wildlife sanctuary is filled with trees and flowers and a couple of small ponds. Located on Bone Hill Road, there are two entrances to Long Pasture. The first is a small, rocky parking lot on the left side, at the first turn of the narrow road. The pathway from this parking area is clearly marked and simple to follow. The second, main entrance is a few hundred yards further at the large white Sanctuary sign on the left; the road will take you to the visitors parking area.

A few hundred feet into the wooded area there is a small open barn with temporary pens used during the warmer months. This area is part of a cooperative effort between the Massachusetts Audubon Society and Ocean Song Farm to attempt something called "Management Intensive Grazing." The farm's pigs, goats, sheep, and turkeys are there to feed on the vegetation at Long Pasture, which is not treated with pesticides. The animals are fun to see, but be careful: the fences are electrified.

The Long Pasture Wildlife Sanctuary Nature Center has extensive views across Barnstable Harbor toward the Sandy Neck Colony and the lighthouse located at the end of the Sandy Neck Trails. The Nature Center is open year-round, offering a variety of experiences depending on the time of day and season of the year.

After visiting the Nature Center, you can return to the parking area at the beginning of Long Pasture by going back the way you came or take the pathway that runs along Bone Hill Road itself. Separated from the road by a short rock wall, the hike back along Bone Hill Road is nearly as quiet and peaceful as the wooded pathway. The road is not busy, even in the summer months, which allows the birds' songs to be heard all around you. The hike does not end there, though.

On the left side of Bone Hill Road, just after the intersection with Harbor Point Road, there are a few perfectly manicured meadows to be walked. In the summer the meadow grasses grow high and the paths become hidden from the roads. In the cooler months the meadows are wide open and easily found.

Important Info:
- Admission: $4 Adult, $3 Seniors and Children Ages 3-12

GOATS AT LONG PASTURE

Long Pasture & View of Sandy Neck Colony
Cummaquid

Sandy Neck
Colony

Parking
area

Long Pasture
Main Entrance

Harbor Point Road

Small
Long Pasture
Parking Area

Bone Hill Road

Route 6A

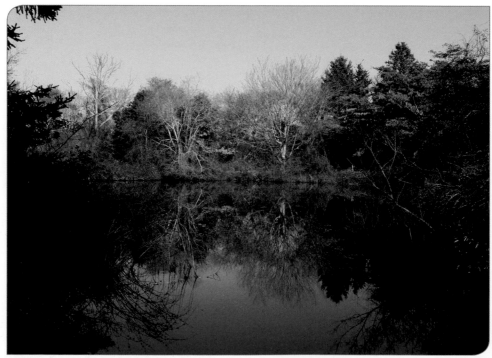

A POND AT LONG PASTURE

3. View of Sandy Neck Colony
Cummaquid

The Sandy Neck Colony is a small group of cottages and a lighthouse located at the tip of the 4,700 acre Sandy Neck Beach. Access to this area is limited to boat travel, off-road vehicles, and those brave enough to walk the seven miles each way in the sand. However, there are a number of places where this small community can be seen and enjoyed from afar.

One is a tiny, sandy parking area at the end of Bone Hill Road, off Rt. 6A, in Cummaquid. This area, next to the Massachusetts Audubon Long Pasture Wildlife Sanctuary, is almost directly across from the cluster of cottages and provides perhaps the best view, aside from being on the opposite shore. This area is quite secluded with room for about four vehicles in the parking area. When the tide is low, one can walk to the edge of the still water and feel like you can almost touch the other shore.

Because of the Sandy Neck Colony, the beach has been designated a historical district. After being shut down since 1952, the lighthouse was recently reactivated in 2007, in time to celebrate the lighthouse's 150th anniversary. It was built in 1857.

Important Info:
• Free but limited parking.
• No lifeguard or concessions

VIEW OF THE SANDY NECK COLONY FROM BONE HILL ROAD.

GPS: (41.701563,-70.275148)

Directions from Previous Site: Follow Bone Hill Road back to Rt. 6A, turn right. The next destination is 300 ft. away on the right, with parking across the street at the Samuel Day Gallery. (Distance: 0.7 mi. Driving Time: 2 mins.

4. The Grave of Iyannough
Cummaquid

Anybody who has been to Hyannis, or the small village of Wianno, has been privy to the influence of legendary Native American "Sachem," or chief, Iyannough. His legend began when the son of Mayflower passenger John Billington wandered away from the new Plymouth Colony in 1621. Iyannough, the Sachem, assisted Governor William Bradford and his party in finding the boy.

Iyannough died young, only in his mid-twenties, in 1623. More than 200 years later, a farmer discovered what is believed to be the grave of Iyannough. There is a simple sign alerting passersby on Rt. 6A of the grave, but few stop or even notice it.

There is a pathway from the road that takes you a few hundred feet to a green dead end where a simple stone has Iyannough's name written on it. It is far enough from Rt. 6A that one can get lost in thought about who rests eternally underfoot. Iyannough is every bit as much a part of the Cape Cod legend as any of the settlers who came here.

Important Info:
• Free parking across the street at *Samuel Day Gallery*

A SIGN FOR THE GRAVE OF IYANNOUGH

THE GRAVE OF IYANNOUGH

III

YARMOUTH PORT

GPS: (41.703752,-70.251064)

Directions from Previous Site: From the parking lot, turn right onto Rt. 6A; follow it 1.2 miles to next destination on the right. (Distance: 1.2 mi. Driving Time: 2 mins.)

1. Hallet's Store

Established in 1889 by Thatcher Taylor Hallet, this Cape institution was originally a pharmacy complete with soda fountain and lunch counter. Now owned by Charles Clark, Thatcher's great-great grandson, Hallet's is still serving ice cream and sodas, while doubling as a museum. The 120-plus year-old shop still has all of its original fixtures inside and, when you sit down to have a sandwich, ice cream, or a soda, you are transported back to the late 19th century. The dedication to retaining authenticity is what makes Hallet's special. It is open from April through November

In addition to the food and beverages, Charles Clark has created a museum upstairs. Focusing on the Hallet family through photographs, objects, and memorabilia, this museum is a reflection a long period in the life of the whole Yarmouth Port community. It is a great experience to enjoy some refreshment and history at this legendary Cape Cod institution.

Important Info:
• Free Parking on Rt. 6A

HALLET'S STORE

GPS: (41.705136,-70.244121)
Directions from Previous Site: Continue on Rt. 6A for 0.4 miles to next destination on left.
(Distance: .4 mi. Driving Time: 1 min.)

2. Winslow Crocker House

Originally built in 1780, this house was originally located in West Barnstable. The owner was a wealthy trader and land speculator named Winslow Crocker. In the 18th century, the home stood against the backdrop of surrounding farms.

It was bought and moved to its present site by Mary Thacher in 1936. The move was slow and painstaking, taking over ten months to travel a distance of six miles. Ms. Thacher subsequently used the house to showcase her collection of colonial furniture, hooked rugs, ceramics, and other antiques.

Today, set back from the road with a spacious yard, the house appears as it did when it was originally built. A lush green lawn leads the eye across the yard to the front of the historic home. It has the appearance of a beautiful painting, especially on bright and sunny days.

The Winslow Crocker House is available for tours and operates as a museum where many of Mary Thacher's antiques are still on display. It is opened on the second and fourth Saturdays of each month from June 1st through October 15th.

Important Info:
• Admission: Adults, $4

WINSLOW CROCKER
HOUSE

3. Captain Bangs Hallet House

In an area filled with historic homes, this is one that stands out. Built in 1840, and named for an illustrious 19th century fisherman, it is the only historic house that is regularly open to visitors. Tours of the house take place often during the summer and fall, but the grounds are always open to walkers. The house itself is preserved as though it were still the 19th century and the Captain was expected to return from a voyage at any time. Interestingly, in 1863, Hallet "swapped" homes with another famous captain, Allen Hinckley Knowles. Captain Hallet and his wife lived in Knowles's house until his death in the late 19th century.

Behind the Bangs Hallet House is a natural wonder: an English Weeping Beech tree that is over a century old. In the warmer months this giant's limbs, covered in broad, flat leaves, reach to the ground. When you step beneath this awesome piece of nature, it feels like you are under an umbrella. Nature lovers and history buffs alike find that the Hallet House is a great place to spend some time.

Important Info:
• Admission: Adults, $3; children, $.50

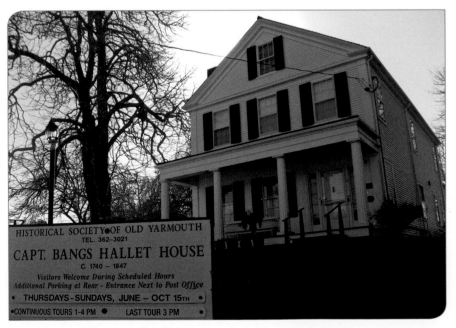

CAPT. BANGS HALLET HOUSE

GPS: (41.722291,-70.234784)

Directions from Previous Site: Take Strawberry Lane it back to Rt. 6A and turn right. Follow it 0.6 miles and turn left onto Center Street. Go 1.2 miles to parking lot of next destination. (Distance: 1.8 mi. Driving Time: 5 mins.)

4. Grays Beach (Bass Hole)

Although formally named Grays Beach, this free, public beach nestled against a narrow cove overlooking Cape Cod Bay is known by locals as "Bass Hole." Its Native American name, "Hockanom," means "hook shaped" and legend has it that the Algonquin Native Americans fought Thorvald Ericson, brother of Leif, in 1003, and killed him here.

Any trip here would have to start with the 800-plus foot long boardwalk that stretches into the neighboring Center Street Marsh. It gives a wonderful view of the bay and Chapin Beach, which acts as a barrier protecting Bass Hole from the harsh ocean waves. The beach area is calm and good for swimming; there are visible sandbars at low tide. A large, open field and a newly revamped playground provide spaces for recreation, and a covered picnic area can be reserved for large parties.

Across from the field are trails that extend through the woods surrounding Bass Hole and across a marsh which, thanks to a recently built walking bridge, gives a great panoramic view of the area. Trails lead through the woods and across Center Street, coming out on the other side of the marsh. There are a lot of biting green-head flies in late-summer, but it should not stop visitors from enjoying one of the few free beaches on Cape Cod.

Important Info:
- Free parking
- Lifeguard in season
- No concessions

GRAYS BEACH SUNSET ON THE BOARDWALK AT BASS HOLE

IV
DENNIS & EAST DENNIS

GPS: (41.733196,-70.231242)
Directions from Previous Site: Follow Center Street back to Rt. 6A, turn left. Follow Rt. 6A 3.3 miles, turn left onto Nobscusset Road, and take 1st left onto New Boston Road. Take a slight right onto Beach Road, follow it 0.9 miles, then take slight left onto Taunton Avenue. Follow it 1.1 miles to parking lot for next destination on the right. (Distance: 6.8 mi. Driving Time: 17 mins.)

1. Chapin Beach
Dennis

Chapin Beach is named for real estate broker George Chapin who gave the land to the town just after World War II. Before it was a public beach, it was known as "Black Flats," for the color of the sand. Today it offers a different sort of thrill: off-roading. The route to Chapin Beach is nearly two-and-a-half miles long, leading to a secluded parking lot, though in summer it is extremely crowded. Those vehicles with the capability may opt to drive along the beach, which extends out to where the Chase Garden Creek Salt Marsh empties into Cape Cod Bay. From there you have a great view of both Sandy Neck in Sandwich to the west and the nearby Grays Beach, also known as Bass Hole, to the east.

Chapin Beach acts as a "barrier beach" for Bass Hole, protecting it from most harsh ocean waves. The drive on Chapin Beach Road is nearly as good as the beach itself. It is a winding, hilly, and sometimes sand-covered journey past beach front homes, with scenic glimpses of Cape Cod Bay. At low tide, the beach allows one to walk up to a mile out onto tidal flats; it is one of the best spots to watch a Cape Cod sunset.

Important Info:
- Daily Parking $20
- No lifeguards
- Concessions
- Dogs allowed Labor Day-Memorial Day

CHAPIN BEACH

GPS: (41.739493,-70.180032)

Directions from Previous Site: From Chapin Beach parking retrace your route 1.8 miles, then turn left onto Whig Street. Take 2nd right onto Hope Lane; cross Rt. 6A onto Old Bass River Road. Follow it 0.2 miles., then take a slight left onto Scargo Hill Road. Follow it 0.6 miles; turn left onto an access road directly across from Doctor Stanton Road. (Distance: 3.4 mi. Driving Time: 12 mins.)

2. Scargo Tower
Dennis

Originally built of wood as an observatory for tourists in 1874, Scargo Tower was named for the legendary Nobscusset Indian, Princess Scargo. She was so beautiful, legend has it, that Indian warriors would come from all parts of Cape Cod to see her and bring gifts to help sustain her people. The original tower was destroyed in a storm two years after it was built; it was rebuilt of wood, but burned to the ground in 1900. The present stone structure was built in 1901.

Standing thirty feet high on top of Scargo Hill, it offers some of the best views of the Mid-Cape area. Cape Cod Bay is easily visible to the north and Scargo Lake lies at the bottom of the hill. The paths down to the lake have been fenced off, but not too many years ago it was possible to scale the hill down to the shore of the lake. On clear days it is possible to see all the way to Provincetown and Plymouth. The tower and its story are unique in an area that should be visited at least once.

Important Info:
• Free parking/admission

SCARGO TOWER

SCARGO LAKE AS SEEN FROM SCARGO TOWER.

GPS: (41.745653,-70.183256)

Directions from Previous Site: Turn right onto Scargo Hill Road and follow it back u to Rt. 6A, taking a slight right onto Old Bass River Road. Turn right on Rt. 6A , follow it 0.7 miles, then turn left onto Osprey Lane and park along the roadside. The next destination is across Rt. 6A. (Distance: 1.6 mi. Driving Time: 5 mins.)

3. Nobscusset Indian Burial Site
Dennis

A little hard to find, but well worth the stop, this gem of history harkens back to the original Native American inhabitants of Cape Cod. The burial site of the Nobscusset tribe, which inhabited in Dennis hundreds of years ago, sits just across the street from Osprey Lane, along Rt. 6A. There is a sign pointing to its location, but it is very easy to miss it and pass by this site all together. There is no parking area for visitors, but the site is not large and will not take too long to see it, so parking along Osprey Lane should be fine.

After walking through a natural tunnel of trees, you come upon the burial ground. The tunnel is remarkable, especially when the sun trickles through the branches. The grounds are fenced and marked by a stone stating that the chief of the tribe was named "Mashantampaine." At the back end of the burial ground, the site offers a view of Scargo Lake, but there are many other places with better access to the lake. This tribute to the original inhabitants of Cape Cod should be seen by all visitors.

Important Info:
• Free but limited parking across the street on Osprey Lane

NOBSCUSSET INDIAN
BURIAL SITE

Nobscussett Indian Burial Grounds
Dennis

GPS: (41.752937,-70.154124)

Directions from Previous Site: Coming out of Osprey Lane, turn left onto Rt. 6A. Follow it 0.3 miles, then take slight left onto Sesuit Neck Road. Just before Bridge Street, continue to follow Sesuit Neck Road as it veers off slightly to the left. Follow it 0.7 miles to next destination, which is on the right. (Distance: 1.7 mi. Driving Time: 7 mins.)

4. Sesuit Harbor
East Dennis

The name of this place and the surrounding areas is sometimes shortened to "Suet." Henry David Thoreau noted it as such in his notes when he passed through between 1849 and 1857. It has also been called "Sissuit" by local Native Americans.

There are two separate but equal sides to this harbor. The west side has the *Northside Marina* and the *Sesuit Harbor Café,* while the east side has prime fishing areas and a short walk to Cold Storage Beach. For better views of the boats coming and going, the east side is preferable. It is easy to spend a warm afternoon enjoying lunch in the parking lot while watching the vessels enter and exit Sesuit Harbor.

On the west side of the harbor, a few beaches, including Harborview Beach with a long jetty, provide a great panoramic views of the harbor on both sides. Sesuit Neck, on the west side, has some picturesque scenery, including a classic Cape Cod cranberry bog. It is worth taking a walk here after seeing the marina and café.

Important Info:
• Free parking

SESUIT HARBOR

GPS: (41.750192,-70.138932)

Directions from Previous Site: Return on Sesuit Neck Road then take the 1st left onto Bridge Street. Turn left on Rt. 6A at the traffic lights. Follow it 0.7 miles, then turn left onto South Street. Follow it 0.7 miles to the next destination. (Distance: 2.4 mi. Driving Time: 8 mins.)

5. Crowes Pasture Beach
East Dennis

Visitors who are not willing or able to take the drive out to the Cape Cod National Seashore, another can have the same experience of untouched Cape Cod at Crowes Pasture Beach. The beach is on South Street in Dennis, just before the Brewster line and past the Quivet Cemetery on the east side of Sesuit Harbor. The road to Crowes Pasture Beach is long, bumpy, and unpaved, it is recommended that you take it slow, or, better yet, have a vehicle capable of four-wheel drive. The scenery is amazing, especially on your first drive out. The 138-acre conservation area has many designated parking areas with views of Cape Cod Bay and the neighboring Quivet Creek Marsh. The popular East Dennis Oyster Farm is located in this area on Quivet Neck. From the designated parking areas, it is possible to walk to the beach or to Coles Pond, which sits in the northeast section of Crowes Pasture and only a few hundred yards from the ocean.

Though it is somewhat hidden, Crowes Pasture is a place where you can easily spend a day enjoying the solitude and beauty of Cape Cod as it was when the first settlers gazed upon it.

Important Info:
- Free upland parking
- Off-road driving pass: $100/resident
- No lifeguard
- No concessions
- Dogs allowed on leash

CROWES PASTURE

V
BREWSTER

1. Drummer Boy Park

This park combines a recreation area with a historical site. Drummer Boy Park is a beautiful, open space that, until mid-2012, was a popular dog park. Dogs are no longer allowed here, but there is a playground for children and some interesting historic buildings to be seen.

First and most obvious is the Higgins Farm Windmill, a behemoth on a hill that is easily seen from Rt. 6A. It was built in 1795 and moved from its previous location nearby on Ellis Landing Road in 1974. It was donated to Brewster by Mrs. Samuel Nickerson in memory of her husband.

On either side of the smock windmill are buildings of historic interest. An old blacksmith shop is on the right. It dates back to 1867, when it was built by Henry Hopkins on his property on Long Pond Road. On the left is the Harris-Black House, built in 1795. It is one of the few remaining one room houses left on Cape Cod. It was moved to Drummer Boy Park from Red Top Road and carefully restored in 1983.

With lots of history and plenty of room for play, this park is a great place for a picnic lunch or to spend an afternoon. There is a nice view of Quivet Creek Marsh on the north side of the park.

Important Info:
- Free Parking
- Dogs are no longer allowed

HARRIS-BLACK HOUSE

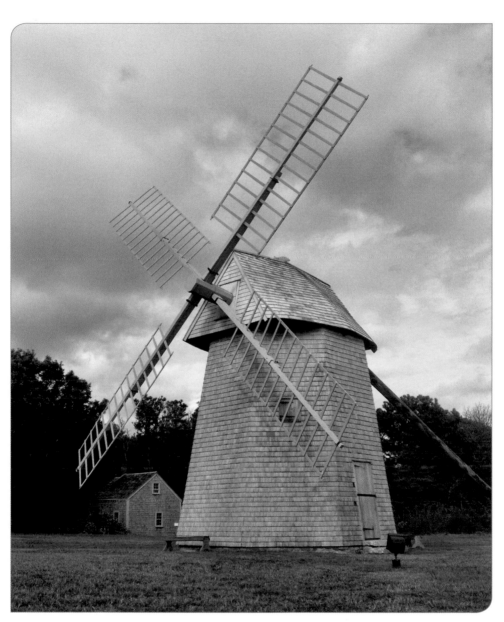

HIGGINS FARM WINDMILL

GPS: (41.753562,-70.115209)

Directions from Previous Site: Turn left on Rt. 6A; follow it 0.1 miles to next destination on the left. (Distance: .1 mi. Driving Time: 1 min.)

2. Cape Cod Museum of Natural History & Wing Island

The Museum of Natural History is filled with amazing exhibits featuring the local wildlife and ecology. It is open every day during the summer and most days during the spring and fall, and is a perfect family destination, being both fun and educational. But it is what is behind the museum that truly makes the trip memorable. It is a living example of what the Natural History Museum's exhibits are all about.

Located across Quivet Creek Marsh, and accessible only at low tide, is Wing Island, named for John Wing, the first white settler to live within the boundaries of what was old Harwich in 1656. To get there, follow the John Wing Trail, which begins as a series of boards across the mucky marsh and leads to Cape Cod Bay. The island trail has several openings which allow a broad view of Quivet Creek Marsh and Cape Cod Bay simultaneously.

The land is filled with birds, butterflies, and sweet smelling flowers during the warmer months, and continues to be an amazing place of natural beauty during the winter.

A parking area in front of the museum gives access to trails on the south side of Rt. 6A that cross a marsh and continue into the surrounding woods. The marsh trail leading to Wing Island is submerged during high tide, so check the charts before heading out there or you may have to slosh your way back to the Museum grounds through two feet of salt water.

This place seems far removed from civilization and is worth the potential for wet shoes.

Important Info:
• Museum Admission: Adults, $10; seniors (65+), $7; children Ages 3-12, $5. The trail to Wing Island is free.

HEADING ACROSS QUIVET CREEK MARSH TO WING ISLAND.

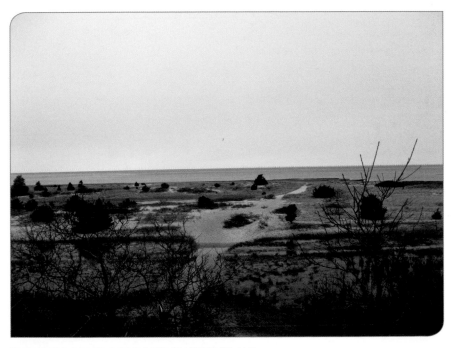

THE VIEW OF CAPE COD BAY FROM WING ISLAND.

3. Stony Brook Herring Run & Grist Mill

Stony Brook Herring Run is a popular site for children and adults alike, especially during the spring herring spawn, when the narrow brook is choked with fish close enough to touch. As tempting as that may seem, taking fish from the grounds is not permitted.

It does not have to be spring to enjoy the herring run. Lower Mill Pond empties through the herring run and continues out into Paine's Creek, and a series "fish ladders," a sort of man-made funneling system for the fish, creates a constant rush of water, overpowering most other sounds. There is an old wishing well on the grounds, and a walking bridge over the brook allows for tremendous views of the natural beauty no matter what season it is.

Across the street from the herring run is the Stony Brook Grist Mill. The original fulling mill was 200 years old when it burned to the ground in 1871; the current mill was built on the original foundation two years later. It houses a museum and is still in operation, despite being 140 years old, so visitors can purchase fresh cornmeal inside. The mill has an amazing wooden wheel affixed to its side, making it a very popular subject for photographers. A search for the mill on the internet produces dozens of photos of the left side of the mill with its large water wheel prominently featured. Behind the mill, you may walk to the stone wall that holds back Lower Mill Pond. The stream leading from this spot to the herring run can be so still at times that it is possible to get a perfect mirror image of the mill reflecting in the water.

Important Info:
• Free parking for Herring Run
• Free admission to Grist Mill

STONY BROOK GRIST MILL

STONY BROOK HERRING RUN

4. Nickerson State Park

Set on 1,900 prime acres, Nickerson State Park houses many kettle ponds formed by glaciers over 10,000 years ago. Campsites offer breathtaking views and the sweet scents of the pine forest that no words can describe. The park bears the name Roland J. Nickerson in honor of the owner of the land in the late 19th century. His mansion is now the *Ocean Edge Resort and Club* in Brewster.

As you a hike around Big Cliff Pond or ride through the eight miles of bike trails, you may feel like you are in the middle of nowhere. In fact, there is a trail located at the far end of Nook Road that comes within a few hundred feet of the Mid-Cape Highway.

Flax Pond and Big Cliff Pond are the most popular places for families to visit. Since none of the kettle ponds have streams or rivers to feed them, their water levels fluctuate from year to year. Just a short walk from the main entrance, Flax Pond has canoes to rent. With no current, the water is very safe and easy to navigate for paddler and swimmer alike.

At the end of Flax Pond Road, you will find Big and Little Cliff Ponds. At their nearest point the two kettles are separated by about seventy-five feet, but they never connect. Canoeing is available here and there are boat ramps available for people coming with their own water transportation. After a short walk up a hill, you arrive at a picnic area with an aerial view of Big Cliff Pond. In summer, the view is obscured by plants and trees. At the top of the hill, there are cabins for camping as well.

Just about any parking area along the whole of the park can be the start of an impressive hike. At Nickerson State Park there really is no bad spot to choose. You will have just as much fun if you point yourself in one direction and just go.

A summer's day at Nickerson would not be complete without stopping at Cobies, a popular restaurant located on Rt. 6A, just before you reach the Nickerson entrance. It has a congenial, casual atmosphere with outside picnic tables and has been serving great fried food since 1948. A visit here can be a perfect way to start or finish your day.

Important Info:
- Free daily admission
- Camping fees (per night): MA resident, $15; out of state, $17
- No lifeguards, no concessions
- Dogs allowed except in swimming areas

NICKERSON STATE PARK

FLAX POND AT
NICKERSON STATE
PARK

LITTLE CLIFF POND
AT NICKERSON STATE
PARK

BIG CLIFF POND AT
NICKERSON STATE
PARK

VI

ORLEANS

GPS: (41.79464,-70.01613)

Directions from Previous Site: Coming out of Nickerson, turn right on Rt. 6A and follow it 1.7 miles. Turn left onto W Street. Continue onto Skaket Beach Road, following it to the parking lot at the end of the road. (Distance: 3.1 mi. Driving Time: 8 mins.)

1. Skaket Beach

Skaket Beach offers beautiful sunset views. Located near the curve of the Cape toward the National Seashore on the north, there are seemingly endless views of the Cape as well. It is easy to see up the coast all the way to Provincetown to the east and, on a clear day, it is possible to see the South Shore of Massachusetts to the west.

The tide is extreme here; when it goes out the beach appears to go on forever and makes for an easy walk a half mile to the west to Namskaket Marsh. Skaket Beach is close enough to Orleans Center and the Cape Cod Rail Trail that it is possible to spend the entire day there, have a nice dinner nearby, and return to watch an incredible sunset. The parking lot is not large and fills up fast on summer days, especially with spillover from nearby Nauset Beach, so get there early to enjoy the water and the views.

Important Info:
• Daily parking: $15
• Lifeguards and concessions in season

SKAKET BEACH

GPS: (41.799439,-70.007569)

Directions from Previous Site: Follow Skaket Beach Road 1.1 miles to Rock Harbor road and turn left. Continue 0.5 miles to the next destination on the left. (Distance: 1.7 mi. Driving Time: 5 mins.)

2. Rock Harbor

A beautiful place for a swim or a sunset photo, Rock Harbor is unique. In the summer, what a visitor notices first are trees spaced out into the harbor to help guide boats into the harbor. This odd sight may cause you do a double take, but this is part of Rock Harbor's charm. Typically, the trees are adorned with regular street signs to reflect the lights of incoming vessels. The trees are removed during the winter.

Walking the beach to the west will take you to a salt marsh, while an eastern walk will take you to Boat Meadow. For those looking for an adventure on the water, fishing charters are run out of Rock Harbor. It is a popular area for watching the sunset, with the sun dipping below the waters on Cape Cod Bay. There is plenty of parking.

During the War of 1812, this was the site of a British attack that was thwarted by the Orleans Militia. The ship HMS *Newcastle* sat offshore with the intent of burning the village and its vessels, but was repelled by the soldiers from Orleans.

In the harbor is the historic CG36500 Motor Lifeboat, built in 1946. This vessel is famous for rescuing the thirty-two man crew of the tanker *Pendleton* during a dangerous winter nor'easter in February 1952.

Important Info:
• Free Parking

THE TREES AT ROCK HARBOR

CG36500 MOTOR LIFEBOAT AT ROCK HARBOR

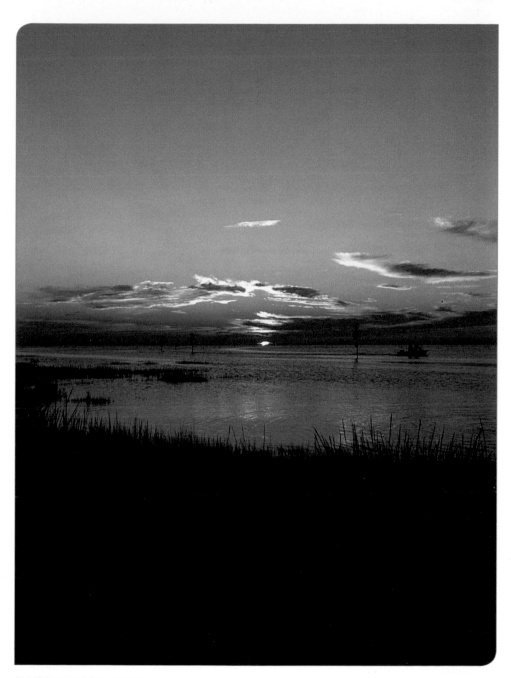

SUNSET AT ROCK HARBOR

GPS: (41.788577,-69.936971)

Directions from Previous Site: Follow Rock Harbor Road 0.9 miles and continue onto Main Street, following it another 1.8 miles. Take a slight left onto Beach Road and follow it 1.4 miles to the parking lot of Nauset Beach. (Distance: 4.1 mi. Driving Time: 11 mins.)

3. Nauset Beach

Named for the Native American tribe that originally inhabited the area, Nauset Beach is one of the best spots to surf on the East Coast and one of the most popular beaches on the Cape. Located where Nantucket Sound and the Atlantic Ocean collide, Nauset Beach has some rough seas and large waves. Even when the tide is low the waves here are larger than anywhere else along the shores of Cape Cod. Even if you are not a surfer or don't like to swim, taking a walk along Nauset Beach is a must. In the summer, the large parking lot fills up quickly, so it is wise to make a journey to Nauset Beach as early as possible.

Listening to waves and watching them crash on the shore is a soothing, almost meditative experience. If you are walking and lose yourself in the moment, you may look up and suddenly find yourself miles from the parking lot.

Many of the east-facing Cape beaches are visited by seals, dolphins, and other marine animals. Seals are the most plentiful, but there is no guarantee that you will see one bobbing up and down in the water, though it always possible when the weather is warm.

Nauset Beach is also one of the best spots to watch the sunrise.

Important Info:
• Daily parking: $15
• Lifeguards and concessions in season
• Dogs: From a point south of Nauset Beach parking lot to Trail One, dogs are prohibited from May 15 to Labor Day. From a point south of Trail One to the Chatham Inlet, all dogs must be on a leash of not more than 30 feet at all times, unless below the high tide mark, from May 15 through Labor Day. Dogs are prohibited from areas closed to vehicle or human traffic for Piping Plover protection

CROSSING THE DUNES TO NAUSET BEACH

NAUSET BEACH

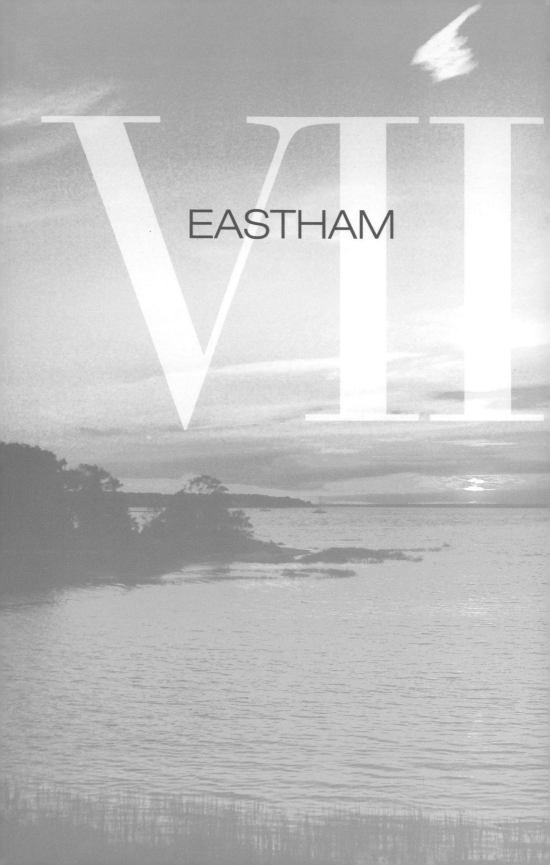

VII

EASTHAM

GPS: Fort Hill (41.818152,-69.96206)
Penniman House (41.818704,-69.965552)
Directions from Previous Site: From Nauset Beach follow Beach Road 1.4 miles, turning slightly right onto Main Street. Follow it 1.2 miles, turn right onto Rt. 28, and follow it 1 mile. Take first exit on rotary for Rt. 6. Follow Rt. 6 1.4 miles, then turn right onto Governor Prence Road. Turn right onto Fort Hill Road, follow it 0.1 miles. The parking area for the next destination is on the left. (Distance: 5.4 mi. Driving Time: 12 mins.)

1. Penniman House & Fort Hill

Built in 1867 by whaling Captain Edward Penniman, Penniman House is a testament to the fortune he gained through seven successful whaling voyages. His love for whaling is depicted by the pair of whale ribs acting as a trellis over the entry to the front yard. Situated among some more contemporary homes along Fort Hill Road, the Penniman House stands out, with its red and yellow colors and Second Empire-style architecture. The Second Empire style, including some French elements, was popular mainly from 1865-1880. This was the first house in town with indoor plumbing. Captain Penniman lived here until his death in 1913.

After a stroll around the grounds of this marvelous mansion, it is only a short drive to the lookout area of Fort Hill. There is a panoramic view of Salt Pond Bay and the Atlantic Ocean, with a trail that leads down to the water and back toward the Red Maple Swamp. When standing at the overlook to the north, you can see all the way to Coast Guard Beach, where the large, white Coast Guard building sits high on a hill. On warm days, the ocean breeze makes the trail walk amazing. On cold days, it can be tough, but the views are worth the potential shivers.

Important Info:
• Free parking at Fort Hill
• Penniman House admission is free, but donations are appreciated

PENNIMAN HOUSE

THE VIEW FROM FORT HILL

GPS: (41.830705,-69.974781)

Directions from Previous Site: Follow Fort Hill Road to Rt. 6. Turn right and go 0.9 miles. Turn left onto Samoset Road. Parking for the Windmill Park is on the right. (Distance: 1.1 mi. Driving Time: 4 mins.)

2. Windmill Park

Easy to pass without notice, Windmill Park is home to the oldest windmill on Cape Cod. Now across from the Town Hall on Rt. 6, this windmill was originally built in Plymouth in 1680 by Thomas Paine of Eastham. It was subsequently moved to Truro in 1770, to Eastham in 1793, and, finally, to its current home in 1808. There is a gazebo behind the windmill along with a stone trough that is over a hundred years old. The water pump is locked, but the trough is a nice supplement to the windmill. Its inscription, "Blessed Are The Merciful," is a positive message to take from the park.

The windmill sits near the back of the park, so is a piece of history that can be overlooked as people drive by on the main road at forty miles per hour. It is worth the stop though. It is also possible to see the windmill from the Cape Cod Rail Trail, which passes just to the west of Windmill Park. The park is used for events such as craft fairs and concerts during the warmer months.

Important Info:
• Free parking on either side of the park along the roads

WINDMILL PARK

GPS: (41.837627,-69.972743)

Directions from Previous Site: Continue on Rt. 6, following it 0.5 miles, then turn right onto Salt Pond Road. The next destination is on the right. (Distance: .7 mi. Driving Time: 3 mins.)

3. Salt Pond Visitors Center, National Seashore

Though the Cape Cod National Seashore contains more than 43,500 acres of incredible forest, dunes, and coastline, the actual gateway to the Seashore is the Salt Pond Visitors Center. It is open every day from 9 a.m. to 4:30 p.m., with longer hours during the summer. Inside people can learn what the Seashore is all about, through films and an extensive museum. The Salt Pond is located down a short trail behind the center.

From the Visitors Center, a short trip by car, bike, or foot takes you to Doane Rock and Coast Guard Beach. As an alternative, the Nauset Bike Trail, only 1.6 miles in length, also goes down to Coast Guard Beach. For walking, the Nauset Marsh Trail, which is 1.5 miles, is very popular and easy to navigate. One can access the Cape Cod National Seashore through countless roads and beaches, but beginning a journey into this untouched area of natural beauty at the "gateway" at Salt Pond makes it feel more special.

Important Info:
• Free Admission

SALT POND VISITOR'S CENTER

GPS: (41.843958,-69.957907)

Directions from Previous Site: Continue on Salt Pond Road, which becomes Doane Road, for 0.8 miles, then turn right onto Pinecrest Drive. The next destination is on the left. (Distance: 1 mi. Driving Time: 3 mins.)

4. Doane Rock

A part of the National Seashore, Doane Rock is a deposit left behind by glaciers and is the largest exposed boulder on the Cape. Roughly fifteen feet high, it is a reminder of one of the early Cape Cod families. Deacon John Doane settled in Eastham in 1644 and was a holder of many local government offices before settling Eastham. He was so influential that his name was even mentioned by Henry David Thoreau in his writings about Cape Cod in the mid-19th century.

The boulder can be climbed, of course, and around the boulder there are trails leading throughout the Seashore. A short walk from Doane Rock takes you to the site of the Doane Homestead, marked by the granite memorial and a small, square clearing. It is impressive that more than 350 years ago an original Cape Cod family lived on that spot. Perhaps this is especially true for me because they are my ancestors, but one does not have to be related to the Doanes to appreciate it any history lover will enjoy it.

Important Info:
• Free admission and parking

DOANE ROCK

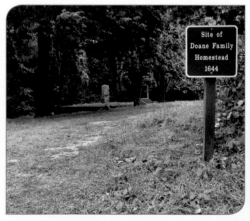

SITE OF THE DOANE HOMESTEAD

GPS: (41.859461,-69.952551)

Directions from Previous Site: Turn right onto Doane Road and follow it 0.6 miles, continuing onto Ocean View Drive. Follow this for 0.9 miles. Parking for the next destination is on the right. (Distance: 1.6 mi. Driving Time: 4 mins.)

5. Nauset Lighthouse

Originally part of the Chatham Twin Lighthouses, Nauset Light is located on a hill overlooking Nauset Light Beach. It was built in Chatham in 1877 and moved to Eastham in 1923. Before this, the Three Sisters Lighthouses guarded the shore for passing vessels. This cast iron giant was dismantled in 1993, when the rapidly eroding cliff where the lighthouse stood required that it be moved 300 feet west, where it currently stands. It was saved through a tremendous effort by the Nauset Light Preservation Society (NLPS), which was formed in 1993 by a group of concerned Eastham residents. Since its inception the group has contributed substantial amounts of money toward the moving and restoration of the lighthouse; the society now numbers more than 800 members in forty states.

During the 1940s, the Nauset Lighthouse was painted red and white to match its red and white beacon; its color scheme has made it possibly the most well known lighthouse on Cape Cod. Views of the lighthouse from Nauset Light Beach, and vice versa, are simply magnificent. During each of my visits I try to find one new, unique angle of Nauset Light and have not been disappointed yet. There is no shortage of photo opportunities at this historic site. It is open on Sundays from July through October.

Important Info:
- Parking is at Nauset Light Beach
- Daily parking: $10
- Lifeguards in season, no concessions
- No dogs allowed May 15 to Labor Day

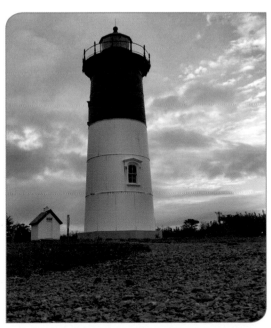

NAUSET LIGHTHOUSE

6. The Three Sisters Lighthouses

The "Three Sisters" lighthouses can easily be missed by travelers, as they are not located on the shores of Cape Cod, but are spaced across an open field down the road from Nauset Light Beach. Their story may be the most amazing of all of the Cape lighthouses, but it also may be the least known.

THE THREE SISTERS LIGHTHOUSES

The diminutive Three Sisters, each standing only fifteen feet tall (as opposed to the forty-eight foot tall Nauset Light), originally sat overlooking Nauset Light Beach, as far back as 1838. In 1892, the original brick lighthouses were replaced with these wooden structures. After being removed during the 1920s to make way for the Nauset Light, which had been brought up from Chatham, the Three Sisters were separated. The National Park Service repurchased them one-by-one, and in 1983, after 73 years apart, the Sisters were reunited in the field where they currently stand. They were restored and placed at the same distance apart that they had been when they watched over the Atlantic. Only the middle Sister, the last one that stood over Nauset Light Beach, still has its lantern adorning its top; there was not enough funding to repair the lantern rooms on the other two.

Parking is very limited at the field on Cable Road, where the lighthouses stand. It is easier to park either at the nearby Nauset High School or at Nauset Light Beach and walk to where they stand. They are worth the hike.

Important Info:
• Parking: There is room for a few cars in front of the lighthouses, or park at Nauset Light Beach (daily parking, $10)

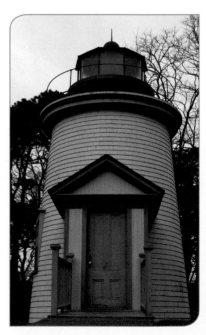

THE MIDDLE 'SISTER' OF THE THREE SISTERS LIGHTHOUSES.

WELLFLEET

GPS: (41.878045,-69.987999)

Directions from Previous Site: Continue on Cable Road, following it 0.7 miles and turning right onto Nauset Road. Follow this 0.9 miles, then turn right onto Rt. 6. Continue 0.8 miles. The next destination is on the left. (Distance: 2.6 mi. Driving Time: 7 mins.)

1. Wellfleet Drive-In Theater

A relic harkening back to a different era, the *Wellfleet Drive-In* is one of only 368 active drive-in movie theaters left in the United States. At the peak of their popularity in the late 1950s, between 4,000 to 5,000 drive-ins were operating in the U.S. As recently as the early 1980s, there were a handful of drive-ins on Cape Cod, including theaters in Dennis, Yarmouth, and Hyannis. The Dennis drive-in site is now overgrown with trees and brush, the Yarmouth drive-in site is an open field, while the Hyannis drive-in site is now the Independence Drive shopping center. The original entrance to the Hyannis site is still evident, as it runs behind the former Borders Bookstore and is designated by a row of trees evenly spaced to the right of the building.

With a 100' x 44' screen, the *Wellfleet Drive-In* has been in operation since 1957 and is open from late-May through Labor Day. The soundtrack can be played directly through your car stereo radio, or, if you want a real trip down memory lane, you can hang the mono speaker on your window. Whether reliving their own childhood or seeing a drive-in movie for the first time, this is an experience that visitors must try. You will not forget it.

Important Info:
• Parking is free
• Tickets for shows are as follows: Adults, $8; seniors (62+), $5; children (under 12), $5; children 3 and under are free
• Concessions

THE WELLFLEET
DRIVE-IN

GPS: (41.893732,-70.001711)

Directions from Previous Site: Coming out of the drive-in, turn left onto Rt. 6 and follow it 1.5 miles. Turn left onto Lieutenant Island Road and continue 1.4 miles to the next destination. (Distance: 3 mi. Driving Time: 8 mins.)

2. Lieutenant Island

Lieutenant Island is a little south of Bound Brook Island in Wellfleet and accessible only at low tide. The island, it is said, was named for Lieutenant Anthony, a 1600s Native American who lived at Billingsgate on Wellfleet Harbor.

A bridge passes over the marshy area and, although this bridge is slightly elevated, the surrounding land is underwater at high tide. When you plan your visit, be sure to check tide charts; it would be easy to become stranded on the island side. Because dirt roads can be treacherous, it is better to hike across the bridge or take a bicycle if you do not have an appropriate vehicle. There is a small parking area before the bridge, so it is possible to park and walk. Wetlands along the south side of the island are connected to the Massachusetts Audubon Society. The island is open to shellfishing from, October through May.

Lieutenant Island is filled with summer homes, but can be virtually deserted during the off season. It is quiet and secluded in the colder months, with beach views of Loagy Bay to the east and Cape Cod Bay to the west. The views and trails for hiking are superb and can be enjoyed no matter what the season.

Important Info:

• Free parking in a few designated areas. There is a small parking area at the end of Way 100, the first road on the immediate left. There is another small area on Pond Ave., on the right just before the private roads begin. Otherwise you may walk across the marsh road at low tide to the island.

LOOKING BACK FROM
LIEUTENANT ISLAND

GPS: (41.912825,-69.972709)

Directions from Previous Site: Follow Lieutenant Island Road back out to Rt. 6, turn left. Follow it 0.3 miles; turn right at the lights onto Marconi Beach Road. Turn left onto Marconi Station Road and follow it 0.9 miles to the next destination. (Distance: 2.9 mi. Driving Time: 9 mins.)

3. Marconi Station & White Cedar Swamp

Part of the National Seashore, the Marconi Station site honors Guglielmo Marconi who, in 1901, oversaw the building of the first transatlantic wireless telegraph station. In 1903, at a place not too far from the current site, President Theodore Roosevelt sent a radio message across the Atlantic to King Edward VII of England. The station was also one of the first to receive radio distress calls from the *Titanic* after it struck the iceberg in 1912.

There is a platform on a hill near the Marconi Station that offers a wide view of the Atlantic Ocean and the National Seashore lands surrounding the Marconi site. Originally, four 210-foot tall wooden towers stood in a square around the transmitter building. Due to heavy erosion of the cliffs, however, the station remained operational for only sixteen years and was closed and dismantled in 1917.

This is an inspiring place for historians. A small scale model of the original Marconi Station, makes it possible to imagine the giant towers, visible from all around Wellfleet. During the spring of 2011, after a rash of severe storms, a pair of bases of the original Marconi Station towers were revealed on the beach below. They are accessible by walking a little more than a mile from Marconi Beach. It is amazing to see the steel and wood from a hundred years ago still intact after spending over a century under the water and sand.

As awe-inspiring as the Marconi site, scale model, and revealed tower bases may be for historians, there is a place that produces the same feeling for nature lovers just across the parking lot. A mile-long hike into the sandy pine forest will lead you to the White Cedar Swamp which seems so out of place along the beaches and ocean. The land leading up to the swamp is typical Cape Cod terrain, but the White Cedar Swamp seems to appear from nowhere. A boardwalk takes you through the area, where trees block most of the sun, allowing only trickles of light to splash through to the water. It has a dusky feeling even in midday, and is strange and beautiful. This is one of the most highly recommended places to visit on all of Cape Cod.

Important Info:
• Parking is free

WHITE CEDAR SWAMP

THE MARCONI STATION
SITE

ONE OF THE ORIGINAL
BASES OF THE MARCONI
WIRELESS TOWERS.

4. The Site of the Chequesset Inn

One of the most fascinating places to visit on the Cape may seem like just another slice of ocean, but the story of what once stood on this spot is a remarkable piece of Cape Cod history. The Chequesset Inn was an exclusive luxury resort built in 1902, on the 400-foot Mercantile Wharf. With sixty-two rooms, the resort helped make Wellfleet tourist destination. In 1934, the rough waters of the harbor claimed the Chequesset Inn, when a cold winter filled the harbor with ice chunks that ravaged the pier's pilings and caused the Mercantile Wharf to collapse during a storm. The Inn was taken down shortly thereafter, along with the pier.

There is a marker on the curve of Kendrick Avenue designating where the Mercantile Wharf jutted out into the harbor. To the east is Mayo Beach and to the west are the Wellfleeter Condos. An awe-inspiring feeling comes over you at the edge of the water, knowing what was there seventy-five years ago. At low tide it is still possible what remains of the pilings that once made up Mercantile Wharf. A trip to this spot should coincide with low tide, or you will not see anything but water. Make it here at the right time and you will catch a glimpse of history rising from the shallows.

Important Info:
• Free parking in a small turnoff (room for one car). Also parking available at Mayo Beach, where daily parking is also free.
• Dogs allowed Oct. 16th to May 31st

THE SPOT WHERE THE OLD CHEQUESSET INN ONCE STOOD.

GPS: (41.933133,-70.069198)

Directions from Previous Site: Continue left on Kendrick Avenue, which becomes Chequesset Neck Road. Follow it 1.7 miles; parking for the next destination is on the left. (Distance: 2 mi. Driving Time: 5 mins.)

5. Billingsgate Shoal

Billingsgate was once a small island community located a mile south of Jeremy Point. In the 17th century, Billingsgate Island was approximately sixty acres in size. At one point in the mid-1800s, the island had thirty homes, a schoolhouse, a lighthouse, and even a baseball team. The lighthouse was originally built in 1822 and rebuilt twice before finally being destroyed by erosion in 1915.

The erosion of the island was exacerbated when the inhabitants removed the trees that held the land together, and allowed their livestock to graze, removing much of the beach grass. Around the time of World War I, the island was virtually deserted because of the extensive erosion, and many of the structures were floated off the island and resituated in Wellfleet, Brewster, and West Barnstable. Today all that remains of Billingsgate Island is a large sandbar at low tide with pieces of the lighthouse foundation and a scattering of bricks still visible.

Billingsgate's remains are accessible at low tide and the area is large enough for shellfishing and picnicking, but that's about it. The legend of this once thriving island community still lives in Wellfleet, as many of the island's homes ended up there. It is said that some of the former Billingsgate homes can be found Holbrook Avenue near Wellfleet Harbor, although some of these may be from Bound Brook Island near Wellfleet. The guessing is half the fun. The only building that certainly was once on Billingsgate Island now stands as part of the *Wicked Oyster* restaurant at 50 Main Street in Wellfleet, as is mentioned in its history.

It is not easy to get there, but visiting Billingsgate Shoal at low tide will have you standing, quite literally, on a piece of vanishing history with an incredible, sad tale that reminds one of the wrath of the sea.

Important Info:
• Parking at Great Island lot is free
• No lifeguards
• No concessions

Billingsgate Shoal
Wellfleet

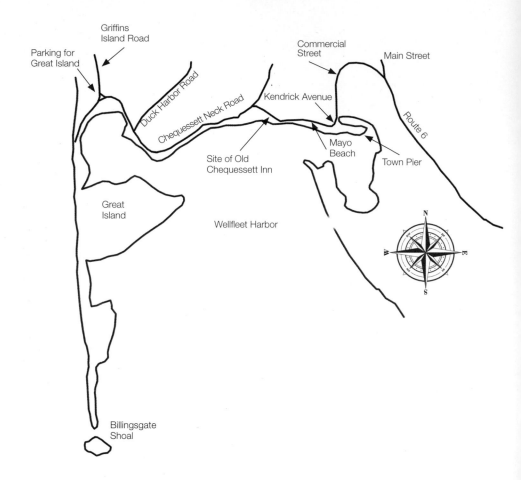

Griffins
Island Road

Parking for
Great Island

Duck Harbor Road

Chequessett Neck Road

Commercial
Street

Main Street

Kendrick Avenue

Route 6

Site of Old
Chequessett Inn

Mayo
Beach

Town Pier

Great
Island

Wellfleet Harbor

Billingsgate
Shoal

GPS: (41.950953,-70.074224)

Directions from Previous Site: Turn right onto Chequesset Neck Road and left onto Duck Harbor Road. Follow it 1 mile, then turn right onto High Toss Road. After 0.5 miles continue onto High Toss Bridge Road, and turn left when it ends at Pole Dike Road. Take a slight left onto Bound Brook Island Road. Follow it 0.8 miles, keep left at fork in road, and continue 1 mile to next destination. (Distance: 4.3 mi. Driving Time: 11 mins.)

6. Bound Brook Island

Though not really an island, Bound Brook Island is another hidden gem on the Outer Cape. This picturesque area of the National Seashore has an scenic beach, but getting to it is difficult. The journey starts with Bound Brook Island Road off of Rt. 6. It is unpaved and uneven, so it might be better to park and walk or bike to it, if you do not have a four-wheel drive vehicle. The surface of the road is a few feet below grade, making it feel like you are driving down a chute. There are very few places to turn around until the small beach parking lot.

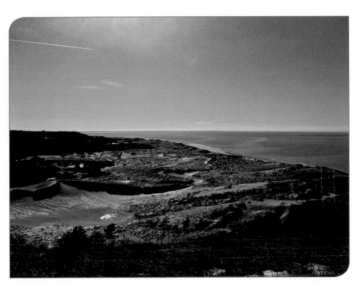

BOUND BROOK ISLAND

Once you make it to the beach, though, your effort will seem worthwhile. There is a sandy pathway leading over the dunes to a beach with a broad view across Cape Cod Bay. On a clear day, it is possible to see straight across to Plymouth and other South Shore communities. While the view from the shore is amazing, the best view of all is from a sloping sandy hill near the beach at the end of Bound Brook Island Road. A path leads to its summit, which is over seventy feet high. From there you will feel as though you can see from Provincetown to Maine. This view by itself makes the tough trek to the beach a mere footnote. The large dune is not a climb for everyone, but the view from the sandy pathway to the beach is nearly as good for those who do not wish to attempt the dune.

Important Info:
- Limited free parking
- No lifeguard
- No concessions
- Dogs allowed Oct. 16th to May 31st

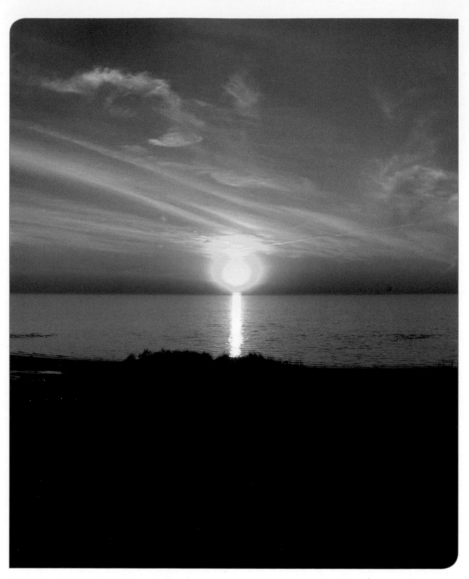

SUNSET AT BOUND BROOK ISLAND

IX

TRURO

1. Pine Grove Cemetery

For travelers who crave the darker side of Cape Cod, this place will easily suffice. Pine Grove Cemetery, remotely located more than a half mile from any homes, is the scene of perhaps the most horrific crimes ever committed on Cape Cod: The Antone Costa Murders.

The murders occurred in 1968 and included mutilation and dismemberment of several young girls' bodies. The murderer was Antone Costa, who became the subject of a book entitled *In His Garden,* written by Leo Damore. Costa died in his prison cell in 1974, by hanging himself.

The cemetery was the subject of paranormal research in 2007, with a few odd occurrences happening to the investigating team, although nothing overwhelming. The most interesting area they encountered was a small 8x8 foot crypt at the rear of the cemetery. The crypt was once used to house bodies during winter, when the ground was too cold for them to be buried. It was in this half-circle-shaped brick structure that Costa purportedly dismembered the bodies and possibly even cannibalized them.

When I visited the cemetery at dusk on a misty, foggy afternoon, I spent some time inside the crypt. Mysteriously, my cell phone battery die in an instant, which I am told was due to a spirit using surrounding energy to manifest itself.

Even if you are not daring enough to sit where such terrifying crimes took place, the cemetery is a historical footnote and a quick drive by the crypt can't hurt....can it?

Important Info:
• Parking is free

THE CRYPT AT PINE
GROVE CEMETERY.

PINE GROVE CEMETERY

Pine Grove Cemetery
Truro

2. Pamet Harbor

Pamet Harbor is considered one of the birthplaces of the American Whaling industry. The harbor is named for the tribe of Native Americans that inhabited the land at the time of the arrival of the first European settlers. Near the end of the Pilgrims' voyage, there was a stopover in what is now Truro. The Pilgrims and Pamet Tribe fired upon one another, but nobody was killed. Soon after, the Pilgrims sailed off and landed in Plymouth.

The land was purchased from the Pamet Tribe in 1689, and became known as Truro in 1709. Known for farming until the early 19th century, whaling soon became a central part of life. The harbor and the whaling industry in Truro boomed, until a great storm destroyed the fishing fleet in 1841. After a brief revival that lasted into the 1860s, the town quieted down and remains a quaint village to this day.

Truro's harbor has beautiful scenery, including the Pamet River, Pamet Marsh, and the beach area. The *Pamet Harbor Yacht & Tennis Club*, located adjacent to the harbor, should be visited during a trip to Truro.

Important Info:
• Parking is free
• No lifeguards
• No concessions
• $10 fee for boat launching

PAMET HARBOR

GPS: (42.038441,-70.065792)

Directions from Previous Site: Follow Depot Road 1.2 miles, then take a slight left onto Truro Center Road. Take the 2nd right onto Old Pamet Road, then turn left onto Rt. 6 and follow it 2.4 miles. Turn right onto S. Highland Road, continuing on it for 1.3 miles. Turn right onto Highland Light Road. The lighthouse is straight ahead. (Distance: 5.3 mi. Driving Time: 12 mins.)

3. Cape Cod or Highland Lighthouse

Highland Light, which is surrounded by the *Highland Links Golf Course*, is the oldest lighthouse on Cape Cod. The first Highland Lighthouse was built in 1797. The current tower was finished in 1857, and is the third lighthouse built near this site. In 1996, when erosion brought it to less than a hundred feet from the edge of the 120 foot high cliff, the current lighthouse was moved back 453 feet to save it from possible collapse.

The lighthouse has two names. The National Oceanic and Atmospheric Administration (NOAA) lists the lighthouse as Cape Cod Light, while locals

HIGHLAND LIGHTHOUSE

know it as Highland Light because it resides in the "highlands" of Truro. From the lighthouse looking south, one can see several structures that are on the grounds of the defunct *North Truro Air Force Station*. Although it is no longer operational, this is considered government property and cannot be explored.

A stone marks the spot where the lighthouse sat until its move in 1996. Today, the stone cannot be more than fifty feet from the edge of the of the bluff, which confirms just how necessary the move was. The lighthouse is owned by the National Seashore and managed by the non-profit group *Highland Museum and Light, Inc.* Views of the shore below and across to Provincetown are amazing, and should be experienced by every visitor to Cape Cod.

Important Info:
- Parking is free
- Concessions at Highland Links Snack Bar
- Tours of lighthouse mid-May to mid-October
- Admission: $4

HIGHLAND HOUSE, TRURO

GPS: Montano's GPS (42.044966,-70.095827)
Gravesite GPS (42.051332,-70.093483) (*this is an approximation*)
Directions from Previous Site: Turn right onto S. Highland Road, then take the 1st left onto Highland Road, following it to Rt. 6. Turn left onto the exit ramp toward Provincetown and follow Rt. 6 for 1.2 miles; the next destination is on the right. (Distance: 2.3 mi. Driving Time: 5 mins.)

4. The Grave of Thomas Ridley
North Truro

Thousands of people pass by Montano's Restaurant on Rt. 6 in North Truro every year, but it is what lies deep in the woods behind Montano's that is of interest here...if you can find it: the grave of Thomas Ridley. Thomas Ridley died of smallpox in 1776. He was a fisherman who had ten children with his wife Elizabeth. After he died his body was taken deep into the North Truro woods and buried far from civilization, for fear of the deadly disease spreading. His wife lived to be 74 and was buried Provincetown Cemetery Number 1.

Montano's Restaurant is the jumping off point for this adventure, but only a handful of people, including myself, have ever successfully found this grave. It is barely more than a foot tall and a foot wide, and is surrounded by trees, brush, and debris, masking it almost entirely from anyone not right on top of it. Directions leading to the stone itself are difficult to give. There is a sandpit located a few hundred feet behind Montano's, to the northeast. It is said that, if you find the sandpit, you have a fighting chance to find the grave.

From the sandpit, take a right turn following an overgrown fire road. In these woods, there are many kettle holes left by receding glaciers; it is the second kettle hole on the left that you are meant to circumnavigate. Go around the right of this kettle hole and between two others, where you go left. As you head back toward the beginning, you should nearly trip over the grave. It is hardly an easy task.

The truly adventurous should definitely try their hand at finding a place that so few have ever seen or even know about. Just beware it is easy to get lost in these woods.

Important Info:
• Parking at Montano's Restaurant is free

MONTANO'S
RESTAURANT,
N. TRURO

THE PATHWAY TO THE SECRET GRAVE
OF THOMAS RIDLEY.

THE GRAVE OF THOMAS RIDLEY

GPS: (42.055238,-70.117123)

Directions from Previous Site: Turn right onto Rt. 6, follow it 1.3 miles, then turn right onto High Head Road. Follow it 0.3 miles up a hill; the next destination is on the left. (Distance: 1.7 mi. Driving Time: 3 mins.)

5. Pilgrim Lake
North Truro

This is an area that hundreds of thousands of people pass by each year, but only a very few stop to see the lake. It is named for the Pilgrims who skirted along the shores here, on their way across to Corn Hill. In the 17th century the lake was a harbor.

Pilgrim Lake is located on the eastern side of Rt. 6, just before Provincetown. It is bordered by huge sand dunes and is part of the National Seashore. The lake looks impressive, even when passing it by at more than fifty miles per hour. However a quick turn onto High Head Road leads to one of the most breathtaking views on the entire Cape.

High Head Road quickly goes uphill, leading to several places that overlook the lake. In 2004, the tidal flow was restored to Pilgrim Lake, thanks to a man-made culvert connecting it to the eastern side of Provincetown Harbor. There is a dirt parking area at the base of the hill on High Head Road, where a walking trail takes you around some of the lake area. Hiking is a good option, but the views from up above, on High Head Road, are most impressive. There are also picturesque views of Pilgrim Lake a short drive south, at Pilgrim Heights, along a walk on the Pilgrim Springs Trail.

Important Info:
- Parking is free
- No lifeguard
- No concessions

PILGRIM LAKE

PROVINCETOWN

GPS: Herring Cove Beach (42.046281,-70.216854)
Race Point Lighthouse (42.062337,-70.243075)
Directions from Previous Site: Follow High Head Road back to Rt. 6, turn right, and continue 3.9 miles. Turn right onto Race Point Road. Follow it 1.6 miles, then turn left onto Province Lands Road. Follow it 0.9 miles; a parking area for the next destination is on the right. (Distance: 6.6 mi. Driving Time: 12 mins.)

1. Race Point Lighthouse

This amazing area can be accessed one of two ways: from Race Point Beach or from Herring Cove Beach. The easier route is from Herring Cove Beach, where the Province Lands Bike Trail begins. Race Point Lighthouse, built in 1876, sits roughly a mile and a half from the Herring Cove Beach parking lot, and the view is worth the walk.

The paved bike trail that winds through the tall sand dunes is like a different world. A very scenic dirt road that forks off toward the lighthouse on the left features a beautiful marsh on the left and the Provincetown Municipal Airport on the right. Small planes occasionally pass overhead breaking the otherwise quiet atmosphere.

It is faster to drive to the lighthouse, but an off-road permit is required. Besides, standing before Race Point Lighthouse after completing the full walk is even more satisfying. This is the tip of the Cape, with the entirety of it stretching out behind you. From May through October the lighthouse keeper's house, as well as the beautifully renovated brick Whistle House are available for rent by the day or week.

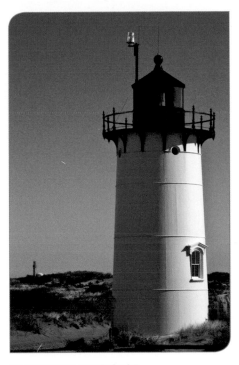

RACE POINT LIGHTHOUSE

With nothing but the sound of the ocean waves crashing all around, it is easy to lose track of time while standing in the shadow of Race Point Light, and that is not a bad thing. The name "Race Point" refers to the strong cross currents that occur here at the very top of the arm of Cape Cod.

Important Info:
- Parking along Province Lands Road is free. There is also parking at Herring Cove Beach: daily fee, $10
- Lifeguard and concessions in season
- Province Lands Road Parking GPS (42.061861,-70.217262)

THE LIGHTHOUSE KEEPER'S HOUSE.

THE VIEW OF RACE POINT LIGHTHOUSE FROM ACROSS THE MARSH.

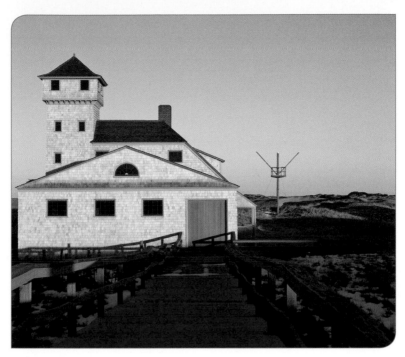

OLD HARBOR LIFE-SAVING STATION AT RACE POINT.

NATIONAL PARK SERVICE BUILDING AT RACE POINT.

2. Province Lands Bike Path

Not as long or as well known as the main stretch of the Cape Cod Rail Trail, this seven-and-a-half mile bike path has some of the most beautiful, unspoiled scenery one could hope to see on Cape Cod. Beginning at Herring Cove Beach, the path includes several offshoots. The elusive Race Point Light is located down a dirt road adjacent to the path and is a worthwhile walk. Plus, there are many views of the nearby Pilgrim Monument, which towers above the dunes and pine trees. Some of the sand dunes rise twenty to thirty feet into the air, adding to the splendor of the ride and giving the bike path a secluded feel.

The path ends at Race Point Beach, the northern most point on the Cape, which should be explored, if time permits. You do not need to be ride a bicycle; this is an amazing place to walk or run as well. Though much of the trails is sand, there are some spots with tree cover, including the Beech Forest. It is possible to see a traditional cranberry bog among the 4,000 acres of the Province Lands area. In 2009, the path was improved, including widening and resurfacing two-and-a-half miles of the asphalt. This has made the experience even better for all riders, runners, and walkers.

Important Info:
- Parking is at Herring Cove Beach. Daily parking $10.
- Lifeguard and concessions in season

PROVINCE LANDS BIKE PATH

GPS: Wood End Light GPS (42.021245,-70.193504)
Long Point Light GPS (42.033138,-70.168627)
Directions from Previous Site: Exit the Herring Cove Beach parking lot, turn right onto Rt. 6A.
Continue 0.9 miles, continue onto Province Lands Road. Parking for the next two destinations is
at the circle. (Distance: 1.3 mi. Driving Time: 4 mins.)

3. Wood End Lighthouse

Though not quite as difficult to reach as Race Point Light, getting to Wood End Lighthouse is an exercise in determination if it is to be seen up close. Parking can be at a premium at the beginning of Province Lands Road, so that is the first step to accomplish. The next step is a walk across the nearly one-mile long breakwater that stretches across the western edge of Provincetown Harbor. The breakwater is fairly level, but the distance discourages people. The journey to the lighthouse is one to remember. About halfway across the breakwater, turn around and take a look at the spectacular Pilgrim Monument looming high above the rest of Provincetown.

Built in 1872, Wood End Lighthouse sits stoically among the small dunes and beach grasses. As at Race Point Light, standing before the white stone rectangle is quiet and peaceful. At forty-five feet tall, it is hard to miss from the street and if you turn to the left there is another white rectangle further down the beach: Long Point Lighthouse.

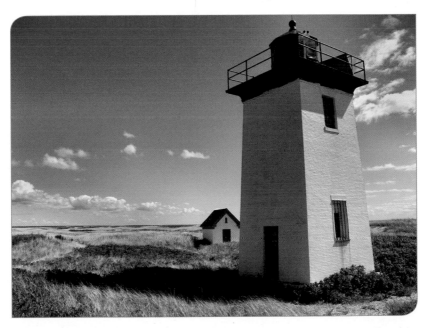

WOOD END LIGHTHOUSE

4. Long Point Lighthouse

Located a little more than a mile-and-a-half from Wood End Lighthouse, this nearly identical light station was built shortly after a settlement was formed in 1818. At its peak, the settlement held nearly 200 people. Some of the houses built during the time of that settlement were floated from the end of Long Point across to Provincetown's West End; they are designated by plaques.

From the tip of Long Point, there is a clear view across Provincetown Harbor to where Rt. 6 and Rt. 6A come up from the south. You can also make out a few of the collections of identical cottages that line the water in North Truro.

This may be the most isolated lighthouse on the Cape and very few people have the desire to walk a mile along a breakwater and then another mile-and-a-half on the sand to reach it. Once there, it is as if you are alone in the world.

There is a small dune next to the lighthouse with a wooden cross on top. The cross is adorned with a tattered American flag and a name plate which reads: "Charles S. Danby: 'Gallant Soldier,' Killed In Action Oct. 17, 1944"

Long Point Lighthouse is a place that many have seen, but few have been in its shadow. Give it a try.

Important Info:
• There is free but limited parking at the end of Commercial Street

LONG POINT LIGHTHOUSE

THE WOODEN CROSS NEAR LONG POINT LIGHTHOUSE.

GPS: (42.0522,-70.188627)

Directions from Previous Site: Drive around the circle heading north on Province Lands Road. Turn right onto Bradford Street Extension, and follow it 1.1 miles. Turn left onto Winslow Street, slight right at High Pole Hill Road to arrive at the next destination. (Distance: 1.5 mi. Driving Time: 5 mins.)

5. Pilgrim Monument

PILGRIM MONUMENT

Standing 252 feet high, and perched atop High Pole Hill, the point of Pilgrim Monument is 350 feet above sea level, making it a prime destination. It commemorates the Pilgrims' first landing place on their journey from England to America in 1620. The Pilgrims spent five weeks exploring the tip of the Cape before heading across the bay to Plymouth. While they were here, on November 11, 1620, they signed the Mayflower Compact, which was the first document of the democratic society in the New World and the original governing document of Plymouth Colony.

The inside of the monument is unique. Etched in some of the granite blocks on the climb are the names of many towns across the United States that donated stones for the monument. The cornerstone was laid in 1907 by President Theodore Roosevelt and the tower was dedicated by President Taft three years later. It celebrated its 100th anniversary in 2010.

From the top, the view is nothing short of spectacular. All of Provincetown is clearly visible, as is the National Seashore area leading down the "arm" of the Cape toward Orleans and Brewster. On a clear day, it is possible to see across Cape Cod Bay toward the South Shore, Plymouth, and Boston. The sixty ramps and 116 steps it takes to climb the Monument should not deter anybody from enjoying this landmark.

Important Info
• Parking is free for 2 hours with paid admission
• Admission: adults, $10; seniors (62+), $7; students 15 & older w/ID, $7; children (4-14), $4; children 3 & under, free

VIEWS OF PROVINCETOWN
FROM THE TOP OF THE
PILGRIM MONUMENT.

XI

CHATHAM

GPS: (41.671357,-69.949352)
Directions from Previous Site: Head back out to Bradford Street, turn left. Follow it 0.6 miles, and turn left onto Howland Street. Follow it 0.4 miles; take a slight right onto Rt. 6. Follow it 25 miles to the Orleans rotary. Take the 3rd exit at rotary for Rt. 6A. Follow it 0.7 miles, turn left onto Rt. 28, then follow it for 8.5 miles. Continue onto Shore Road, follow it 1.2 miles, then continue onto Main Street and follow it 0.4 miles. Parking for the next two destinations is on the left. (Distance: 36.8 mi. Driving Time: 56 mins.)

1. Chatham Lighthouse

A part of the Coast Guard station, Chatham Lighthouse was originally built in 1877, but the station itself was established in 1808 under orders from President Thomas Jefferson. For 115 years the Chatham Light station consisted of two lighthouses, then one of the lights was moved to Eastham where it became Nauset Light. The remaining light stands majestically overlooking North Beach and the view from the sand looking up at the lighthouse is spectacular.

The original Chatham Light lantern and lens were removed in 1969 and are currently on display at the historic Atwood House, a short drive away on Stage Harbor Road. The lighthouse is not open to the public except for special tours during the warmer months, but the view of this Cape landmark is spectacular from just beyond the fence as well.

Important Info:
• Parking is available across the street at North Beach; daily parking $15
•GPS (41.671357,-69.949352)

CHATHAM LIGHTHOUSE

GPS: (41.671357,-69.949352)

Directions from Previous Site: Directly across the street from Chatham Lighthouse.

2. North Beach

North Beach is located near the end of Main Street in Chatham, directly across from Chatham Lighthouse, and is a continuation of Nauset Beach in Orleans. The beaches can be observed easily from the elevated parking lot, which also has three sets of powerful binoculars to aid in viewing.

The story of the formation and destruction of this beach is every bit as interesting as any Cape Cod story. Up until 1987, the beach had been known as a "barrier beach" and continued down toward Monomoy Island. Then, a huge winter storm caused a break in the beach directly opposite of Chatham Light, which eventually widened and caused the loss of seven North Beach cottages. A second break occurred in 2007 a little further north and the initial break has now widened to nearly two miles. This is a fascinating story of the ocean versus the land.

The beach is quite popular during the summer, with the inner harbor area, caused by the break in the beach, being used as a starting point for windsurfers. Even though there has been much erosion to North Beach, it is still a large and popular recreational area. It is located roughly twenty feet below the surface of the road, which is why the views looking down on the beach are so unusual.

Important Info:
• Daily parking $15, though there are spots reserved for looking and not for going to the beach, those are free for 30 minutes
• No lifeguard
• No concessions
• Dogs allowed Labor Day-Memorial Day

NORTH BEACH

SUNRISE AT NORTH BEACH

GPS: (41.657672,-69.958777)
Directions from Previous Site: Follow Main Street southwest, take a slight left onto Morris Island Road,taking the next right to stay on Morris Island Road. Follow it 0.8 miles and continue onto Tisquantum Road, following it 0.2 miles. Turn left onto Wikis Way; the next destination is on the left. (Distance: 1.3 mi. Driving Time: 3 mins.)

3. Monomoy National Wildlife Refuge

Located a short drive from Chatham Light, down Morris Island Road, this 7,600 acre wildlife sanctuary is filled with natural beauty, perfect for sightseeing and school field trips. It is a great spot to spend the day with the family. Even the drive out to the Wildlife Refuge is filled with beautiful scenery. Monomoy is the only designated wilderness area in southern New England; most of the acreage was set aside as such in 1970. The name "Monomoy" is believed to come from the Algonquin Tribe's word "munumuhkemoo" meaning "there is a rushing of mighty water."

Visitors will find a trail that leads along the high cliffs and has a great view of the northern portion of Monomoy Island. There is a weather radar station behind a fence along the trail as well. A set of stairs leads down to the beach and, seemingly, to the end of the civilized world. Once you start to walk south, there is complete solitude, except for the occasional passing of small fishing boats into the harbor. It is a very relaxing walk, as the rushing waves and salty breezes melt away any conscious thoughts. The walk along the beach ends with a panoramic view of Monomoy Island, which, at low tide, sits only a few hundred feet offshore. The remainder of the walk leads west to Stage Harbor Lighthouse, across the mouth of the harbor.

Monomoy Island can be accessed by boat; the lighthouse is on the southern half of the island. This is the only reminder of any past human habitation on Monomoy. There are daily excursions to Monomoy for seal watching or to take a walk on the island.

Important Info:
• Parking is free

MONOMOY WILDLIFE
REFUGE, CHATHAM

GPS: (41.673365,-69.965654)
Directions from Previous Site: Head back out to Tisquantum Road, turn right, and continue onto Morris Island Road. Follow it 0.8 miles, turn right to stay on Morris Island Road, then follow it 0.2 miles. Turn left onto Bridge Street, follow it 0.8 miles, and turn right onto Stage Harbor Road. Follow it ..3 miles to next destination on the right. (Distance: 2.3 mi. Driving Time: 6 mins)

4. Atwood House Museum

The Atwood House, which is now a museum and the centerpiece of the Chatham Historical Society, is virtually unchanged since it was built by sea captain Joseph Atwood in 1752. Five generations of the Atwood family were raised in the house. The only major change in the historic home is the wing added to it in 1833 by Joseph Atwood's grandson, John, for his wife.

In addition to the Atwood House there are other things to see on the grounds. The museum has nearly 3,000 items of art, decorative arts, maritime artifacts, and more, related to Chatham history, many of them on display.

The Nickerson North Beach Camp also on the grounds, was built in 1947 by Joshua Atkins Nickerson II, a descendent of Chatham founder William Nickerson. Prior to being moved to the museum complex in 1991, it was part of a row of about fifty similar dune shacks found along North Beach before the break in the beach in 1987. In the years right after World War II, you could lug your own materials to the beach and build a dune shack.

On the far side of the parking lot is one of the original lanterns of the Chatham Twin Lights. The Twin Lights consisted of Chatham Light, still standing overlooking North Beach, and a second light which became Nauset Light, when it was moved to Eastham in 1923. The lantern was removed from Chatham Light in 1969 and donated to the Historical Society. With the lantern intact, it is possible to walk around on it and imagine what it was like when this piece of history was guiding ships that came close to North Beach more than forty years ago.

Important Info:
• Admission: adults, $6; students, $3; children under 6 are free

ATWOOD HOUSE MUSEUM

NICKERSON NORTH BEACH CAMP

ONE OF THE OLD CHATHAM LIGHTHOUSE LANTERNS.

GPS: (41.66961,-69.999071)

Directions from Previous Site: Turn right onto Stage Harbor Road; take 3rd exit at rotary for Rt. 28. Follow it 1.7 miles; turn left onto Barn Hill Road. Follow it 0.4 miles; take a slight right onto Harding's Beach Road. Continue into the parking lot for the next destination. (Distance: 3.2 mi. Driving Time: 9 mins.)

5. Stage Harbor Lighthouse

Finding this semi-hidden lighthouse can be another worthwhile Cape Cod hike. To visit it, you need to take a trip to Harding's Beach, which has two parking lots connected by a short road and a fabulous view of Monomoy Island to the east.

Stage Harbor Light is visible from the moment you arrive at the second parking lot, though it is about a mile down the beach. The tower was built in 1880, but the light was deactivated in 1933. The lantern has been removed and the surrounding property is private, but you can get a close look while respecting the boundaries. The removal of the lantern being gave the structure an odd appearance, but it is absolutely a lighthouse.

The pathway to the light is used by vehicles and the walk is much easier than places like Race Point, Wood End, and Long Point Lights. Along with the skeleton of the lighthouse, the original lighthouse keeper's house, a shed, and an outhouse remain on the property. Once you reach the mouth of Stage Harbor, where the lighthouse stands, you should allow time to sit on the sand and enjoy the sounds of the waves.

Important Info:
• Parking at Hardings Beach; daily fee, $15.
• Lifeguards and concessions in season
• Dogs allowed Labor Day-Memorial Day

HARDING'S BEACH

STAGE HARBOR LIGHTHOUSE

6. Forest Beach, The Second Marconi Site

Forest Beach is another in a string of beautiful south facing beaches on Cape Cod. It is a stretch of sand perfect for walking, with great views of Monomoy Island and Stage Harbor Lighthouse. There are also trails that lead you to the nearby Cockle Cove.

It might surprise a lot of visitors and perhaps some locals to find out the historical significance of Forest Beach. Behind the beach in the marshy area, there are four cement pillars in a square pattern that represent the remains of a WCC radio tower used by the Marines. The WCC station was owned by RCA, which bought the equipment from Guglielmo Marconi's company in 1920. The tower, erected in 1948, once stood 300 feet high overlooking the water, and remained there until the land was bought by the town. It is considered by some to be a second Marconi site, though he was not directly involved with it. Not as well known or as directly connected to Marconi as the site in Wellfleet, this site is still historical. The Forest Beach overlook, located behind the marsh area, has a plaque with the historical details.

Important Info:
• Parking is free, but the lot is small, first come first served
• No lifeguard
• No concessions
• Dogs allowed Labor Day-Memorial Day

HOW THE RADIO TOWER LOOKED.

THE RADIO TOWER
BASE AT FOREST
STREET BEACH.

FOREST STREET BEACH

VIEW FROM THE FOREST
BEACH OVERLOOK.

XII

HARWICH

GPS: (41.702172,-70.035494)

Directions from Previous Site: Follow Forest Beach road back out to Rt. 28, turn left, follow it 0.6 miles. Turn right onto Depot Road. Follow it 1.6 miles, turn left onto Queen Anne Road, then take the first right onto Hawksnest Road (formerly Seth Whitfield Road), and follow it in .6 miles to the next destination. (Distance: 3.6 mi. Driving Time: 10 mins.)

1. Hawksnest State Park

The Hawksnest State Park, located off Spruce Road near Exit 11 of the Rt. 6 highway, offers another great, long hike. The large Hawksnest Pond and the smaller Olivers Pond are located within the boundaries of the park. The small, 19th century Head of the Bay Cemetery is located in the northwest portion of the park. Hawksnest Road runs north to south through the forest. There are duck hunting camps on the grounds that date back to the late 1800s.

Hawksnest Road is dirt and somewhat tough to navigate. It might be best to have an off-road vehicle to drive this road. There is only one cabin located in the area and that is private. Hawksnest Camp, a duck hunting area, was founded here in 1925. There were, at some point, at least three other camps in the park area. One is a mass of debris today and the other two were removed, one by the Thompson family when they founded Hawksnest State Park in the early 1950s. A small group called Friends of Hawksnest has begun raising funds to clean up the park and control erosion of the ponds.

Important Info:
- Parking is free in designated areas
- No lifeguards
- No concessions
- Dogs allowed on leashes

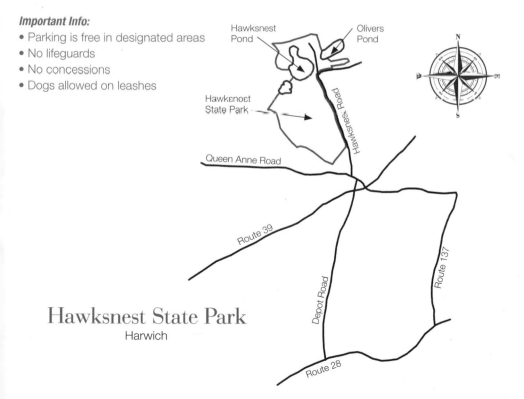

Hawksnest State Park
Harwich

GPS: (41.667679,-70.043229)

Directions from Previous Site: Follow Hawksnest Road back out to Queen Anne Road. Turn left, then take the first right onto Depot Road. Follow it 1.6 miles to Rt. 28. Continue across Rt. 28 onto Uncle Venies Road. Follow it 0.9 miles to the next destination. (Distance: 3.2 mi. Driving Time: 9 mins.)

2. Red River Beach
Harwich Port

The largest beach in Harwich is accessible from three different roads. The Red River, which lies at the eastern end of the long parking lot, marks the border between Harwich and Chatham. From the eastern end of the parking lot there are amazing views of Chatham, Monomoy Island, and Red River. A jetty sticks out forty feet or so into the water, where one can take in all of the breathtaking Cape Cod scenery.

The beach stretches between Red River and Wychmere Harbor. The Wychmere Harbor Club stands stoically at the west end of the beach just across the opening to the harbor. The east end of the parking lot is popular with boaters and kayakers taking short trips across Nantucket Sound to Monomoy Island.

Important Info:
• Daily Parking, $15
• Lifeguards in season
• Dogs allowed Labor Day-Memorial Day

RED RIVER BEACH

GPS: (41.66844,-70.0662)

Directions from Previous Site: Head west along the Red River Beach parking lot to Old Wharf Road, follow it 0.4 miles. Turn right onto Julien Road to Rt. 28 and turn left. Turn left on Harbor Road, or take continue to Snow Inn Road and turn left. Both roads lead to the next destination. (Distance: 1.4 mi. Driving Time: 5 mins.)

3. Wychmere Harbor
Harwich Port

A well-known spot in Harwich, this beautiful harbor can be seen from Rt. 28. It is a spectacular sight as the harbor is downhill from the road, giving one a chance to experience a panoramic view of boats and the ocean. Luckily, on Rt. 28 there is a small dirt turn off at the top of the hill, on Rt. 28, that affords any passers by the opportunity to stop and take a longer, safer look at Wychmere Harbor. On many warm summer days, you may to see several people stopped to take photographs, paint the harbor scene, or simply sitting to take in the scenery.

On the east side of the harbor is Harbor Road, which leads to a marina, where people leave their boats during the warmer months. Here visitors can get closer looks at many vessels, small and large. On the opposite side, sitting on Snow Inn Road, is the Wychmere Beach Club. This popular spot housed Thompson's Clam Bar, a famous Cape Cod landmark, until it closed in 1995. The Beach Club has now come into its own as a beautiful spot for weddings and other outdoor events, thanks to its location on fourteen acres of prime beachfront land.

Important Info:
• Very limited free parking on Rt. 28.

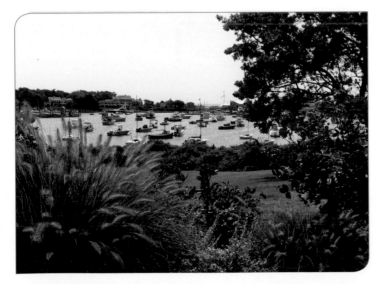

WYCHMERE HARBOR

4. Old Colony Rail Trail

An offshoot of the main Cape Cod Rail Trail, this seven-and-a-half-mile extension takes a rider, walker, or runner from Harwich into Chatham. Named the Old Colony Rail Trail, it honors the abandoned railroad line which the path traces.

This extension of the Rail Trail begins at a rotary in Harwich and ends at Crowell Road in Chatham. It was opened in 2005 and allows you to get acquainted with another section of Cape Cod. Here you will see several ponds, a horse farm, and eventually the Chatham Airport. From the end of the rail trail extension it is a very short trip into the center of Chatham. There is also a "Chatham Loop," which is an extra mile of trail that brings you out to Chatham Lighthouse.

One does not have to travel the entire length, as there are several parking areas along the way for those who wish to cover only a segment of the trail.

Important Info:

• Free parking is available behind the First Congregational Church on Rt. 124.

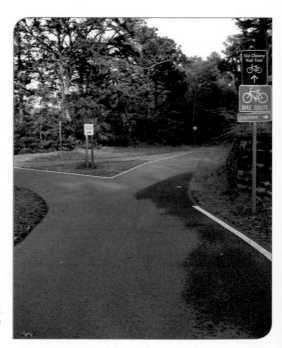

THE ROTARY AT THE BEGINNING OF THE OLD COLONY RAIL TRAIL.

Old Colony Rail Trail
Harwich

Island Pond Cemetery

Rail Trail parking

Old Colony Rail Trail

Old Colony Road

To Chatham

Route 124

Oak Street

First Congregational Church

Route 39

Sisson Road

Forest Street

Parallel Street

Bank Street

To Route 28

N W E S

THE OLD COLONY RAIL TRAIL HEADING TOWARD CHATHAM.

GPS: (41.687792,-70.115574)

Directions from Previous Site: Follow Rt. 124 right back to Rt. 39, turn right, follow it 0.6 miles, continue straight on Main Street, which becomes Great Western Road. Follow it 1.5 miles. Turn left onto Bells Neck Road for the next destination. (Distance: 2.8 mi. Driving Time: 6 mins.)

5. Bells Neck Conservation Area

There are many conservation areas on Cape Cod, some large, some small. At more than 250 acres of natural beauty, Bells Neck is a large conservation area, but it is not very well known outside the local area. It has walking trails, ponds, and an amazing marsh that includes a view of an immense blue water tower hovering above the tree line. There are several entrances into this area. The most widely used is the Great Western Road entrance to Bells Neck Road. Entering this way, you will see the large West Reservoir on the right side. It is nearly always populated by swans and ducks during the warmer months. A main dirt road with several side roads leads to other trails and secluded spots for hiking or enjoying a quiet lunch.

Bells Neck Road continues to Route 28, but there is one side road that should be taken. N Road takes you to the marsh area at Bells Neck and a walking bridge that gives an amazing perspective. The conservation area is in full view from this spot. The muddy area along the marsh river is filled with tiny marsh fiddler crabs that scurry away as you approach.

All the trails are great for walking and the Cape Cod Rail Trail slices through the conservation area as it makes its way from Dennis to Wellfleet. This this short detour gives travelers a quick view of Bells Neck.

Important Info:
• Free parking.

A CLOUDY DAY VIEW OF BELLS NECK.

XIII

WEST DENNIS
& SOUTH DENNIS

GPS: (41.690067,-70.151473)

Directions from Previous Site: Follow Bells Neck Road back to Great Western Road and turn left and go 1.9 miles to the end. Turn right onto Upper County Road. Take the 1st right onto Rt. 134, follow it 0.3 miles to the parking area for the next destination on the right. (Distance: 3 mi. Driving Time: 7 mins.)

1. Cape Cod Rail Trail

The longest of the three recreational paths on Cape Cod, the Cape Cod Rail Trail (CCRT) is a way to absorb the soul of the Cape. At more than twenty miles in length, spanning from Dennis into Wellfleet, the CCRT combines a little of everything that makes Cape Cod beautiful. Many smaller parking areas along the route give even a novice rider or runner access to the Rail Trail without needing to start at the beginning.

The trail winds through the Bells Neck Conservation area in Harwich, over the highway and past a cranberry bog, before sliding past the *Pleasant Lake General Store,* which is a perfect spot to rest and grab something to drink. There are a few ponds along the route for taking a dip on a hot day but the trail is somewhat shaded which does help keep one cooler.

As discussed earlier, the CCRT breaks off near Chatham and also passes through Nickerson State Park, which has its own separate bike path. Once the CCRT passes over the highway again, it begins its ascent into the National Seashore, which can be seen on a bike or on foot. From the trail one can observe Herring Pond, Depot Pond, and Great Pond in Eastham. The Marconi Station site is also on the way in Wellfleet, though it is a bit off the trail.

The main artery of the Cape Cod Rail Trail ends at Lecount Hollow Road in Wellfleet, where is a parking area for those wishing to follow the trail in reverse. Whether you are a novice rider or runner or an expert, or just want a pleasant nature stroll, the CCRT can be enjoyed by anyone, at any point, and at just about any time.

Important Info:
• Free parking at beginning of bike path
• Concessions at beginning of bike path in season.

THE PLEASANT LAKE GENERAL STORE ALONG THE CAPE COD RAIL TRAIL.

THE CAPE COD RAIL TRAIL HEADING UP TOWARD THE NATIONAL SEASHORE.

GPS: (41.690216,-70.15682)

Directions from Previous Site: From the parking area, turn left onto Rt. 134, follow it 0.3 miles, then turn right onto Upper County Road. Follow it 0.2 miles; turn right onto Main Street. Follow it 0.2 miles to the next destination on the left. (Distance: 0.7 miles Driving Time: 3 mins.)

2. Indian Lands & South Dennis Cemetery

Located next to the Dennis Town Offices, the Indian Lands conservation area includes a set of paths that lead down toward Bass River, with a great view of the Highbank Bridge. The master path runs along the power lines and is a tougher hike, with soft sand and stones. The other path follows now defunct railroad tracks overgrown with small trees and plants. There is currently a plan to extend the Cape Cod Rail Trail from Dennis through to Barnstable and the railroad tracks are the route for the new extension. People park at the nearby highway rest area to fish from the banks of the river.

Abutting the parking lot is another piece of history called either Old South Dennis Cemetery or Dennis Ancient Cemetery. It lies behind the Town Offices in a fenced in area, but is accessible. The gravestones bear some of the names long associated with Cape Cod, like Baker, Bangs, and Nickerson. Walking past these stones is like a crash course in Cape Cod history, reminding visitors and residents alike of who came before them.

Important Info:
• Free parking

THE ENTRANCE TO THE SOUTH DENNIS CEMETERY.

THE ENTRANCE TO THE INDIAN TRAILS.

BASS RIVER ALONG THE INDIAN TRAILS.

3. Wilbur Preserve, North & South
South Dennis

Cape Cod's many conservation areas include some smaller ones that are hidden gems, known only to a scant few people. One such place is the Wilbur Preserve North located in the historic district of South Dennis off Farm Road.

A little finger of land sticking out into Bass River, Wilbur Preserve North has limited parking, but there are usually open spots. The tiny beach is at the bottom of a hill and there are some great scenic views of the river and surrounding houses from the top of that hill. This can be a very peaceful, secluded area to enjoy an afternoon. The fact that it is relatively unknown helps keep it so.

Wilbur Preserve South is a few hundred yards away on Cove Road. It is also a finger of land, but has a boat ramp at the end of the road. This is the better known of the two Wilbur Preserves, but each is unique and they are equally enjoyable.

Important Info:
- Free Parking at both locations
- No lifeguards
- No concessions.

WILBUR PRESERVE
NORTH

Atop a hill
overlooking
Bass River
from Wilbur
Preserve North

Wilbur Preserve North & South
Dennis

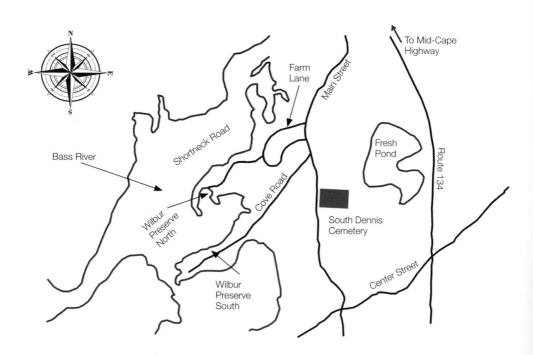

GPS: (41.651238,-70.175797)

Directions from Previous Site: Follow Cove Road back to Main Street. Turn right, continue 0.7 miles, then bear right onto Old Main Street and merge it onto Rt. 28. Turn left onto School Street (becomes Lower County Road , and follow it 0.6 miles. Turn right onto Lighthouse Road. Stay to the right onto Davis Beach Road, then take the 2nd exit off the rotary to the next destination. (Distance: 3.9 mi. Driving Time: 10 mins.)

4. West Dennis Beach

With nearly a mile and a half of pristine sand between Bass River and the neighboring Lighthouse Inn, West Dennis Beach is a very popular south-facing beach in the Mid-Cape area. The long parking lot is perfect for walking or running, and there is even an area designated for kite surfing. The jetty that stretches into the water at the west end of the beach is used for fishing, but also gives one a great view of Bass River and across the water to Smuggler's Beach. About a mile off shore is a small rock cluster used as a destination for boaters or swimmers to relax away from the crowds. Before beginning an excursion out to it, remember that it looks closer than it is.

THE MOUTH OF BASS RIVER FROM WEST DENNIS BEACH.

At the eastern end of the beach a smaller parking area gives access to a new series of man-made sand dunes, built, complete with beach grass and fences, to protect and the beach from the ravages of erosion and help replenish it. For those visiting for the first time, the "new" sand dunes will appear as a natural part of the environment.

On the north side of the parking lot, a marsh has many beautiful homes located across it. When the tide rises, there are many perfect photo opportunities, with the calm water acting as a mirror. The marsh water eventually runs further east and empties into Uncle Stephans Pond, located among more summer homes and rentals. Despite the size of the parking area, West Dennis Beach is packed on most summer days, so it is wise to arrive early—which gives you more time to enjoy this amazing beach.

Important Info:

- Daily parking, $20
- Lifeguards and concessions in season
- Dogs allowed Labor Day-Memorial Day.

SUNSET AT WEST DENNIS BEACH

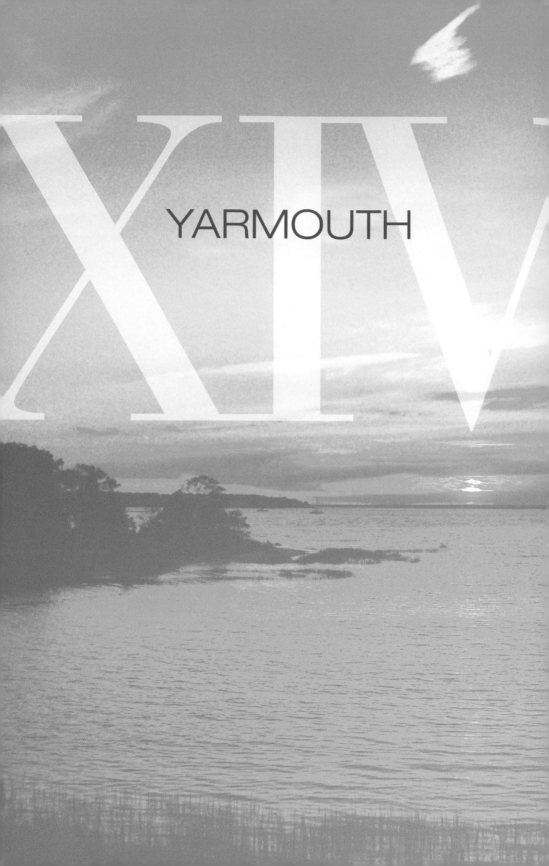

XIV

YARMOUTH

GPS: (41.670336,-70.191444)

Directions from Previous Site: Take the 2ⁿᵈ exit through the rotary, follow Lighthouse Road out to Lower County Road (School Street). Turn left and stay on School Street to Rt. 28. Turn left, follow it 1.1 miles, and turn right onto Geneva Road. Follow it 0.3 miles to the end, then turn right onto Indian Memorial Drive. The next destination is on the immediate left. (Distance: 3.2 mi. Driving Time: 9 mins.)

1. Indian Memorial
South Yarmouth

A simple memorial of carefully placed stones on the side of Indian Memorial Drive is a sacred place in Cape Cod history, although it seems unassuming to most. Near the memorial, there was once a Native American cemetery situated close to Long Pond. Native Americans were buried on land owned by Robert Howes that was subsequently proposed to be used for a salt works. Their bodies were exhumed and reburied, and later this monument was raised to mark the site of

INDIAN MEMORIAL

the original cemetery. Now a quiet residential street, this is not as well known as some other Native American burial plots. Its story and historical significance deserve to be shared and the memorial should be visited.

Important Info:
• No parking area at memorial but a single car can pull off the road. Parking available at nearby Long Pond Beach, daily rate, $15

Indian Memorial Cemetery
South Yarmouth

Long Pond Beach

Long Pond

Indian Memorial Drive

Station Avenue

N. Main Street

Sharon

Samoset

Wood Road

Indian Memorial

Route 28

GPS: (41.654714,-70.196753)

Directions from Previous Site: Follow Geneva Road back out to Rt. 28 and turn right. Follow it 0.9 miles, then turn left onto Forest Road. After 0.2 miles, turn right onto River Street; follow it 0.3 miles to next destination on the left. (Distance: 1.8 mi. Driving Time: 5 mins.)

2. Judah Baker Windmill
South Yarmouth

Another historic windmill sits on the grounds of the appropriately named Windmill Park on Bass River. Originally built in 1791 by Judah Baker, it was situated in Dennis until 1866, when it was moved to its present location. It was extensively restored in 1999 and now appears as it did when built, more than two hundred years ago. The mill became obsolete with the advent of large commercial mills in the early 20th century.

Windmill Park, on a small parcel of land alongside Bass River, has a very small swimming area and a great view of boats coming in and out from Nantucket Sound. Nearly the entire length of West Dennis Beach is visible across the river from Windmill Park. The windmill is opened seasonally and the Yarmouth Historical Commission is happy to provide a schedule for any interested visitors.

Important Info:
•Free parking

JUDAH BAKER WINDMILL

GPS: (41.635732,-70.225832)

Directions from Previous Site: Head straight across River Street onto Willow Street. Follow it 0.6 miles out to Rt. 28 and turn left. Follow Rt. 28 for 1.2 miles, then turn left onto S. Sea Avenue. Follow it 1 mile, then turn left onto Seagull Road. Proceed to the parking lot of the next destination. (Distance: 3.3 mi. Driving Time: 8 mins.)

3. Sea Gull Beach
West Yarmouth

One of two main beaches on the south side of Yarmouth, along with Smuggler's Beach, Sea Gull Beach is a perfect spot to spend the day. It is bordered on the east by Parkers River and on the west by the private Great Island area. The residents of Great Island are very strict about trespassing, so it is best to pay close attention to the signs designating where the public land ends.

Sea Gull Beach provides a great view of boats entering and exiting Hyannis Harbor, the aircraft coming in and leaving the Barnstable Municipal Airport, as well as Lewis Pond which lies north of the parking lot.

At the end of the large paved parking lot, there is a short dirt road leading to a small parking lot facing Parkers River, where there is ample room for fishing. Being a very popular beach, the parking areas fill up early during the summer. It is wise to plan accordingly if you want to enjoy this spot.

Important Info:
- Daily parking, $10
- Lifeguards and concessions in season
- No dogs allowed

SEAGULL BEACH IN JULY

GPS: (41.657728,-70.259639)

Directions from Previous Site: Follow Sea Gull Road to S. Sea Avenue; turn right and follow it back to Rt. 28. Turn left and follow Rt. 28 for 1.7 miles. Turn right onto Mill Pond Road, parking for the next destination is on the left. (Distance: 3.3 mi. Driving Time: 8 mins.)

4. Baxter Grist Mill
Yarmouth

This piece of history is one of the most viewed spots on the Cape, but probably one of the least noticed. The 300-year-old Baxter Grist Mill sits along a busy section of Rt. 28 close to the Hyannis town line. Thousands of people pass by every day, usually on their way to someplace else. A parking area is located just before the actual mill on Mill Pond Road.

Built in 1710 and named for Thomas Baxter, this corn mill is one of several located on Cape Cod. It is still quite easy to imagine the Baxter family grinding corn for several generations before technology made the mill obsolete around 1900, when electricity and commercial flour became more readily available.

At one time, the mill had a large, wooden water wheel. It was the first site in Yarmouth named to the National Register of Historic Places. Near the parking area, one of the original turbines used in the mill sits among the pine trees and is the only piece of the mill that can be easily touched. There is a chain link fence surrounding the wooden mill, but it is open seasonally for visitors, and the Yarmouth Historical Commission is glad to give a schedule anyone interested in it.

Important Info:
• Free parking on Mill Pond Rd.

BAXTER GRIST MILL

XV

HYANNIS

GPS: (41.640375,-70.279477)

Directions from Previous Site: Turn right onto Rt. 28, follow it 0.5 miles, then take a slight left onto E. Main Street at the lights. Follow it 0.7 miles, turn left onto Ocean Street. Continue 0.8 miles; parking for next destination is on the left. (Distance: 2.2 mi. Driving Time: 7 mins.)

1. Kennedy & Korean War Memorials at Veterans Beach

Located just past the harbor on Ocean Street, Veterans Beach is a great place to spend the day. The Korean War Memorial and John F. Kennedy Memorial are in the Veterans Memorial Park on the beach grounds and provide an extra attraction for visitors. The JFK Memorial consists of a beautiful fountain and a wall with a plaque depicting the late-President's profile. The entire area is surrounded by sweet smelling flowers in the warmer months, including several varieties of roses. The memorial is on a hill, where you can see a panoramic view of Lewis Bay and the boats entering and leaving the harbor.

Beside the JFK Memorial is the spectacular Korean War Memorial. The statue of the American Soldier stands on a pedestal, looking out over the water. A backdrop of flags includes the American flag flanked by the flags of the United Nations, South Korea, Massachusetts, and POW/MIA. It is a great patriotic attraction that needs to be seen on any trip through Hyannis.

Veterans Beach is located next to the Hyannis Yacht Club and is sheltered somewhat from the harsh ocean. On the north side of the beach, a river leads to a pond across Ocean Street. This is a great place to see ducks, geese, seagulls, and even crows and hawks congregating. There are swings for the kids and a nice, shady picnic area. Boats, both big and small, pass by frequently, heading into the harbor or out toward Nantucket or the open ocean. Veterans Beach, with some history mixed in, is a wonderful spot for a fun day.

Important Info:
• Daily parking, $15
• Lifeguards and concessions in season
• No dogs allowed.

KOREAN WAR MEMORIAL

KENNEDY MEMORIAL

THE RIVER NEXT TO VETERAN'S BEACH.

XVI

CENTERVILLE

1. Craigville Beach

One of the most popular beaches on all of Cape Cod, Craigville Beach lies almost in the middle of the southern coast of Cape Cod. The name "Craigville" comes from Dr. J. Austin Craig, who was President of the Christian Biblical Institute until his death in 1881. The beach became popular just after the turn of the 20th century. It is bordered on the east by the smaller Covell's Beach, and on the north by the Centerville river; there are many beautiful private homes along the river. The Kennedy family compound can be seen after a long, eastward walk on the beach. Craigville Beach is

CRAIGVILLE BEACH

a popular starting and finishing point for bike races, road races, and marathons on the Cape and in eastern Massachusetts. It is a warmer water beach, as it faces Nantucket Sound, and is great for swimming. The long stretch of sand makes it a good area to take a peaceful walk during just about any time of year.

Important Info:
Daily parking, $15
Lifeguard and concessions in season
No dogs allowed

CRAIGVILLE BEACH

2. 1856 Country Store

Built in the 1840s as a storage barn for cranberries, this historic store has been a landmark in Centerville for more than 150 years. To this day, the general store sells homemade jams and jellies, soaps, cards, as well as classic penny candies. It is a trip back into childhood for some older visitors and perhaps an introduction to something new for younger visitors.

Despite being a part of Cape Cod for so long, the store is keeping up with the times. It is now possible to purchase items on the their website (www.1856countrystore.com). The little red store has a homey feel to it and a very friendly, accommodating staff. The separate benches outside

1856 COUNTRY STORE

the front door for "Democrats" and "Republicans" are always good for a chuckle. The 1856 Country Store can be a pit stop during a walk on Centerville's beautiful Main Street, or a primary destination. This general store, a Cape Cod institution, is open year-round for all to visit.

Important Info:
• Free parking

1856 COUNTRY STORE

XVIII

COTUIT

1. Loop Beach

With all of the popular and well known beaches on the south side of Cape Cod it is easy to miss some incredible spots. Loop Beach, on Ocean View Avenue, is one that could be overlooked. The road is a one-way loop, giving the beach its name. The beach parking area is not very large and sits at the mouth of Cotuit Bay. The beach is nice, about what one would expect on Cape Cod, but the walk up the hill on Ocean View Avenue gives some most stunning views. The road is dotted with private homes, but several open patches of landscape allow for a view of Cotuit Bay, Oyster Harbors, Nantucket Sound, and the Sampson's Island Sanctuary. The elevation of the road gives a perspective on these areas that is tough to match. The climb up the hill is not difficult or very long, and visitors should take a walk during a break from swimming or relaxing at Loop Beach.

Important Info:
• Free Parking
• Lifeguard in season
• No concessions
• Dogs allowed Sept. 15th to May 15th
Note: It is listed as a 'Barnstable Resident's Only' beach which may restrict it to only year-round residents and those with vacation homes.

THE VIEW FROM OCEAN VIEW AVENUE NEAR LOOP BEACH.

THE VIEW FROM OCEAN VIEW AVENUE NEAR LOOP BEACH.

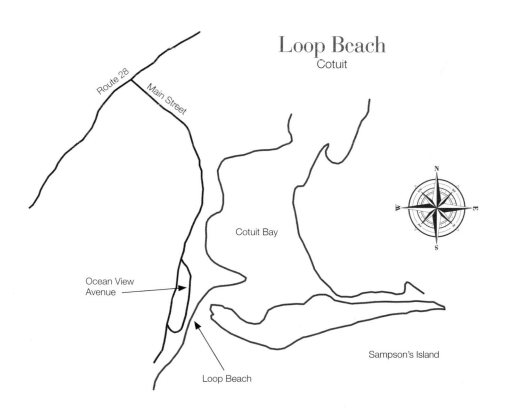

Loop Beach
Cotuit

Route 28

Main Street

Cotuit Bay

Ocean View
Avenue

Loop Beach

Sampson's Island

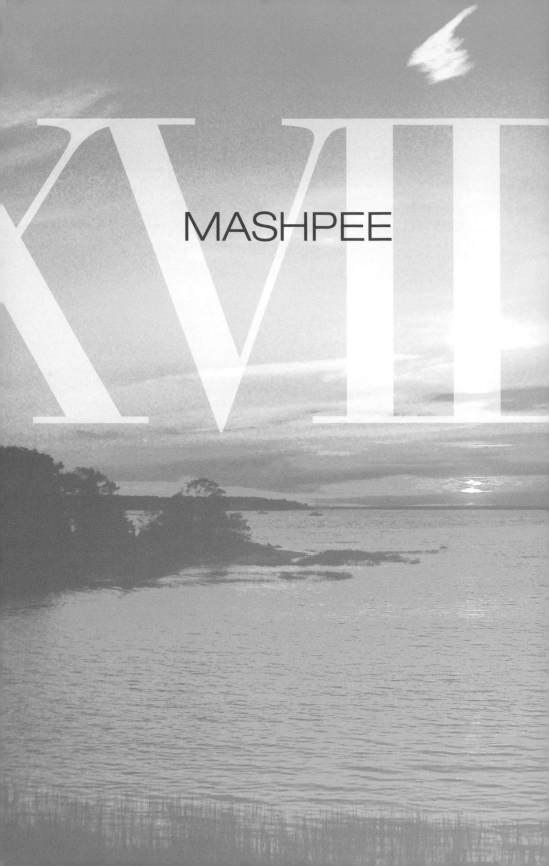

XVIII

MASHPEE

GPS: (41.624902,-70.480117)

Directions from Previous Site: Continue on Ocean View Avenue to Main Street, take a right and go north 0.3 miles. Turn left onto School Street, follow it 0.7 miles, and continue onto Quinaquisset Avenue. Follow it 1.8 miles, turn right onto Rt. 28, then take the 1st left onto Meetinghouse Road. Go 0.2 miles to next destination on the right. (Distance: 3.6 mi. Driving Time: 9 mins.)

1. Old Indian Church

The Native American Wampanoag people are synonymous with Cape Cod. They were here before the first Cape settlements and are still a vital part of the Cape today. For a deeper understanding of the Wampanoags, a visit should be paid to the Old Indian Meeting House, also known as the Old Indian Church.

Built around 1684 as a place for the Wampanoags to practice Christianity, the church is the oldest on the Cape. Though the exact date of its construction is debated, it is rightfully considered one of the most historic buildings on the entire Cape. It is generally thought that the Old Indian Church was moved from its original location in 1717 and relocated to its current site, just off of Rt. 28 on Meetinghouse Road. A cemetery was built on the grounds in the late 18th century and the building once was used as a school.

The church is still used for services by the Wampanoags. After being closed for six years, while it underwent a million dollar renovation, it was reopened in 2009. This Native American church is one of only a few that remain in Massachusetts. It is also one of only a few historic buildings in Mashpee. This is a must-see place for those with a desire to find out more about the original inhabitants of Cape Cod.

Important Info:
• Free Parking.

OLD INDIAN CHURCH

GPS: (41.551996,-70.504271)

Directions from Previous Site: Follow Meetinghouse Road back to Rt. 28, turn right, and go 0.6 miles. Take the 4th exit at the rotary for Great Neck Road South. Follow it 2.8 miles, veering left onto Great Oak Road. Follow this 2.1 miles, then turn left to stay on Great Oak Road. Follow it to the Beach Access Road on the left, and the parking area of the next destination. (Distance: 6.3 mi. Driving Time: 15 mins.)

2. South Cape Beach State Park

This hidden gem of a park is a bit out of the way, but is well worth the trip. The park is relatively easy to find from the Mashpee Rotary. From the parking lot there is a view of Martha's Vineyard across Vineyard Sound, and the beach, but the beach is only the beginning. There are trails through the wooded areas north of the beach, as well as a trail leading between the beach and Sage Lot Pond. Sage Lot Pond is home to swans and

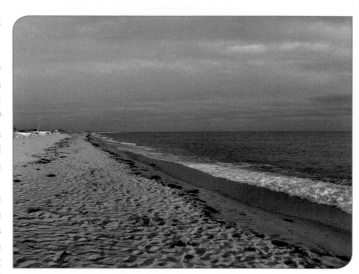

SOUTH CAPE BEACH STATE PARK

ducks, and the path is an easy walk to the State Jetty at the mouth of Waquoit Bay. Boardwalks allow visitors to travel over the dunes without damaging them.

Some who believe that Waquoit Bay was the famed Vinland, the first landing place of Viking Leif Ericson a thousand years ago. For nearly a hundred years, many intelligent minds have been trying to prove just that. But whether it is the first landing spot of the Vikings in North America or not, Waquoit Bay is a beautiful, natural place. From the State Jetty there is a good look across the mouth of the bay to the Washburn Island State Park in East Falmouth.

The park gates are closed from Columbus Day to Patriots Day, but parking can be found at the Mashpee Town Beach at the end of the entrance road.

Important Info:
- Daily admission, $7
- Lifeguards and concessions in season
- Dogs allowed except in swimming areas

SAGE LOT POND

SUNSET AT SOUTH CAPE BEACH STATE PARK.

XIX

FALMOUTH & WOODS HOLE

GPS: (41.542534,-70.61684)

Directions from Previous Site: Turn right onto Great Oak Road, follow it 2.7 miles, and turn left onto Red Brook Road. Follow it 2.1 miles, turn left onto Rt. 28. Follow it 6.9 miles, turn left onto Shore Street, follow it 0.7 miles, then continue onto Surf Drive. Parking for next destination is on the left. (Distance: 12.5 mi. Driving Time: 27 mins.)

1. Surf Drive Beach
Falmouth

There are unexpected historical places on Cape Cod, and one such place is Surf Drive Beach. There are several more popular beaches in Falmouth, but none of carries the connection to America's history that this one does. On these very sands, during the War of 1812, the Massachusetts militia was entrenched after an initial bombardment, preparing for a British landfall that it never came.

The beach is the closest to Falmouth Center and there is a small inlet across the street that usually has some ducks swimming in it. To the east, the Shining Sea Bikeway crosses Surf Drive, and only a little further away is Nobska Lighthouse. This is a fine little beach with historical interest and a convenient location.

Important Info:
- Daily Parking $10
- Lifeguard and concessions in season
- Dogs allowed Oct. 1st to Apr. 30th

SURF DRIVE BEACH

2. Nobska Lighthouse
Falmouth

Originally constructed in 1829, the current Nobska lighthouse was built in 1876 and became a part of the Coast Guard family in 1939. The hill where the lighthouse stands offers a magnificent view of Vineyard Sound, Martha's Vineyard and the Elizabeth Islands.

From the point on Nobska Road, it is possible to see all the way down into Woods Hole to the west, where ferry boats carry passengers out to Martha's Vineyard quite often throughout the day. Because Nobska Light sits on hill, photos of this amazing lighthouse can be taken from many angles, each giving a unique viewpoint. There is also a place across the street that gives a wider perspective of the lighthouse, though care must be taken since it sits at the top of a steep dirt hill leading to the rocky shore below. The grounds of the lighthouse are always open to the public, but the lighthouse itself is on Coast Guard grounds. There are free tours of the lighthouse a few times during the summer and again on New Year's Eve, which is a great time to visit, especially if there is snow on the ground.

Important Info:
• Limited free parking in front of lighthouse.

NOBSKA LIGHTHOUSE

Directions from Previous Site: Continue on Nobska Road west, which becomes Church Street, following it 0.7 miles. Turn left onto Woods Hole Road. Follow it 0.3 miles; take the 1st left onto Crane Street. Take a slight right onto Cowdry Road to the next destination. (Distance: 1.1 mi. Driving Time: 4 mins.)

3. Steamship Authority Ferry to Martha's Vineyard
Woods Hole

From Woods Hole, both Martha's Vineyard and the Elizabeth Islands appear so close that you could reach out and touch them. From the ferry docks, it is barely half-a-mile across the Sound to the coast of the Elizabeth Islands and a little more than two miles to the edge of the Vineyard.

The ships of the Steamship Authority and its predecessors have been sailing the Vineyard Sound waters since 1818. The schedule and rates are reasonable for an island getaway. The typical ferry trip takes roughly forty-five minutes, with at least thirteen voyages beginning from Woods Hole each day, even in the winter.

Another Steamship Authority terminal in Hyannis offers faster access to Nantucket. There are two year-round ports on Martha's Vineyard, at Oak Bluffs and Vineyard Haven, and one on Nantucket. In addition there are several seasonal terminals, including ones in New Bedford, Falmouth, and Harwich, to make travel easier.

Important Info:
• Daily Parking Per Car: Jan 1 to May 14: $8; May 15 to Sept 14: $12; Sept 15 to Oct 14: $10; Oct 15 to Dec 31: $8. GPS (41.522662,-70.669272)

PREPARING FOR AN EVENING VOYAGE AT THE STEAMSHIP AUTHORITY

4. Woods Hole Oceanographic Institute
Woods Hole

Sometimes lost in the majesty of Cape Cod is the fact that it is also home to one of the leading scientific communities on the entire planet. The Woods Hole Oceanographic Institute (WHOI) was established in 1930 and is the largest independent oceanographic institute in the United States.

Many incredible discoveries and historic events have come out of WHOI, including the first manned deep-sea submersible, *Alvin,* which was commissioned in 1964. DSV-*Alvin* is most famous for being the vessel that explored the remains of the *Titanic* in 1986.

WHOI and the Woods Hole community as a whole are open to the public, with many fun and interesting things for visitors to do and see. It is a mix of scientific community, fishing village, and seaside retreat, all of which mesh together seamlessly.

Many small shops and restaurants lining Water Street will keep visitors happy and occupied during their visit—between seal shows at the Woods Hole Aquarium. There is no shortage of entertaining activities in Woods Hole and, of course, Martha's Vineyard is only a short ferry trip away.

Important Info:
• Limited parking on streets with parking meters. It is possible to park in Falmouth and take the WHOOSH trolley into Woods Hole.

WATER STREET IN WOODS HOLE

WOODS HOLE MARINE BIOLOGICAL LIBRARY

LOOKING ACROSS EEL POND TO WOODS HOLE.

5. Julia Wood House
Falmouth

Among the many historic homes to see throughout Falmouth, the Julia Wood House and garden, on Palmer Avenue, is one of the finest. The majestic yellow building that houses the Falmouth Historical Society was built in 1790, for Revolutionary War physician Dr. Francis Wicks. The exquisite garden, located just to the left of the house, can be accessed through a gate in the fence. There is an astrolabe surrounded by flowers on the way in and a sweet cherub birdbath near the middle. The view of the garden from a small gazebo at the back edge is fabulous, especially during the warmer months when sweet smelling flowers are in bloom.

When visiting the Julia Wood House, one has access to the adjacent Hallett Barn, which has a display of many early farming tools. Inside the house, there is the Katharine Lee Bates Room, dedicated to the famed poet and Falmouth resident, who wrote the lyrics to the beloved patriotic song, *America the Beautiful*.

Important Info:
• Free parking
• Tours, $5

JULIA WOOD
HOUSE

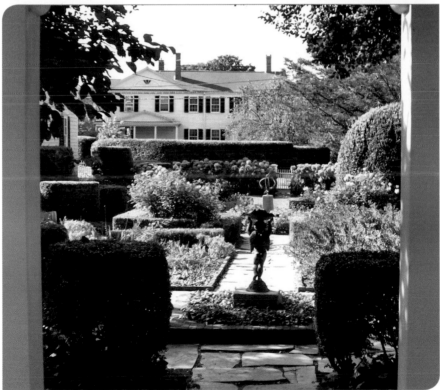

THE GARDEN NEXT TO THE JULIA WOOD HOUSE.

6. Bourne Farm
West Falmouth

Bourne Farm is on the way up Cape Cod's west coast. Established in 1775, it has a spectacular view of the sloping green hill leading down to Crocker Pond in addition to the historic buildings on the property. The forty-nine acre farm is perfect for hiking or walking dogs, and is available for weddings and other events. The farmhouse itself, known as the Crowell-Bourne Farmhouse, was erected by Joseph Crowell and with his father. The Salt Pond Areas Bird Sanctuaries oversees Bourne Farm and handles rentals of the grounds and barn for special occasions. This is a good place to escape for a few hours and is well worth seeking out on your travels.

BOURNE FARM

Important Info:
• Free parking on site.

CROCKER POND
AT BOURNE FARM

GPS: (41.623286,-70.639163)

Directions from Previous Site: Turn right onto Rt. 28A South and follow it 1.3 miles. Turn right onto Old Dock Road, then take the 1st right onto Nashawena Street, following it 0.6 miles, and continue onto Quaker Road. Follow it 1.1 miles; the next two destinations are on the left. (Distance: 3.2 mi. Driving Time: 6 mins.)

7. Old Silver Beach
North Falmouth

Old Silver Beach is possibly the best known place on the west coast of Cape Cod. Located on Quaker Road in North Falmouth, it is popular with locals who fill the parking lot daily during the summer. Two parking areas are on either side of a salt marsh that empties into the bay and a pair of jetties divides the beach in half. The beach is so busy that there is a special lane on the Quaker Road approach that is specifically for the backup of cars waiting to pay to get in during the summer.

The views of the marsh on the east, Buzzards Bay on the west, and the Cleveland Ledge Light in the distance are simply amazing. The lighthouse sits far out in the water, yet peeks over the horizon, due to its immense size. The bayside waters are warmer with stronger currents.

During the 1920s, the University Players—including Margaret Sullavan, James Stewart, and Henry Fonda—performed here for several years. The theatre where they performed burned down in the 1930s.

It is easy to see why so many people plan to visit Old Silver Beach when coming to Cape Cod.

Important Info:
- Daily parking, $20
- Lifeguards and concessions in season
- Dogs allowed Oct. 1st to Apr. 30th

CLEVELAND LEDGE LIGHTHOUSE FROM OLD SILVER BEACH

OLD SILVER BEACH

8. Cleveland Ledge Lighthouse
Falmouth

The last lighthouse built in New England, Cleveland Ledge Light was named for former President Grover Cleveland, who fished the waters of Buzzards Bay. Completed in 1943, the lighthouse sits two miles off shore on a fifty-two feet tall concrete pillar. It was maintained by the Coast Guard, but in recent years was purchased by Sandy Boyd of California, who is planning to restore it to its original condition.

It is best viewed from shore and cannot be climbed. There are several places to see this enormous light station along the Falmouth coast, with the best public views probably from Old Silver Beach.

Important Info:
• Best viewed from Old Silver Beach

CLEVELAND LEDGE LIGHTHOUSE FROM OLD SILVER BEACH

GPS: North End (41.647972,-70.613804)

South End (41.522993,-70.669063)

Directions from Previous Site: Follow Quaker Road north for 1.7 miles; turn right onto Wild Harbor Road. Follow it 0.5 miles, turn left onto Old Main Road, then take the 1st right onto Pine Street. Cross County Road to parking for the next destination. (Distance: 2.5 mi. Driving Time: 5 mins.)

9. Shining Sea Bikeway
Falmouth

A separate, but equally scenic and beautiful, part of Cape Cod's bike trails, the Shining Sea Bikeway takes it name from a line in the iconic "America the Beautiful," written by Katharine Lee Bates, a Falmouth resident. The nearly eleven-mile-long trail was opened in 1975 and is an easy ride. It goes along the shore of Woods Hole into Falmouth, affording riders, runners, and walkers some incredible views of Martha's Vineyard and Vineyard Sound. Once through Woods Hole and Falmouth, the bike trail goes past West Falmouth Harbor, Bourne Farm, and runs close to Old Silver Beach. It ends in North Falmouth where the main parking area is located on County Road, just after Rt. 151.

There are small parking areas along the trail, for those who wish to start where they please. Shining Sea Bikeway may not be as long as the other bike trails on Cape Cod, but the views it offers more than make up for its diminutive length. There is a sense of accomplishment when a rider covers its entire length, which is much easier to complete than the Cape Cod Rail Trail.

Important Info:
• Free parking all along the bike path
• Concessions in season at north and south ends.

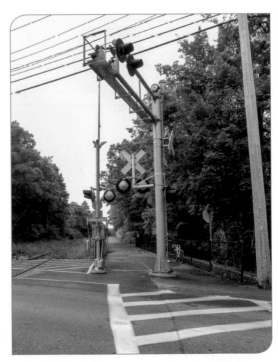

THE SEMI-SECRET BEGINNING OF THE SHINING SEA BIKEWAY ON COUNTY RD.

XX POCASSET

GPS: (41.680773,-70.659133)

Directions from Previous Site: Turn left onto County Road, then left onto Rt. 28A, and follow it 1 mile. Take a slight left onto County Road, follow it 1.1 miles, then turn left onto Shore Road. Follow it 1.5 miles, then turn left onto Barlows Landing Road. Take the 1st right onto Wings Neck Road. Follow it 2.4 miles to next destination. (Distance: 6.1 mi. Driving Time: 15 mins.)

1. Wings Neck Lighthouse

Positioned inches from the water on Wings Neck Island in Pocasset is the Wings Neck Lighthouse, now part of a private home available for vacation rentals. The original lighthouse was built in 1849, but damage from a fire caused a new lighthouse to be built in 1889. The view of the Atlantic Ocean and Buzzards Bay from Wings Neck is incredible. Once the Cape Cod Canal was constructed, water traffic around the Wings Neck Light area increased and it became very important to the safety of traveling vessels near the tip of Wings Neck, which sticks a mile and a half out into Buzzards Bay.

The lighthouse was deactivated in 1945 after the construction of the nearby Cleveland Ledge Lighthouse. It was put up for sale in 1947 and bought by the Flanagan family of Boston. It is a still a private residence and cannot be seen up close unless you are a resident or renting the property for vacation. It can, however, be seen quite well from the gated opening on the edge of the property and is well worth the drive out.

In another interesting twist, the assistant lighthouse keeper's residence, now a private home, was originally a part of Ned's Point Lighthouse in Mattapoisett. In 1923, the house was picked up and floated across Buzzards Bay to Wings Neck.

Important Info:
• Free parking outside the private property.

WINGS NECK LIGHTHOUSE

WINGS NECK LIGHTHOUSE

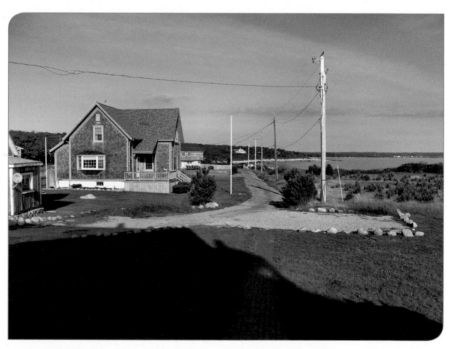

THE ASSISTANT KEEPER'S HOUSE ON THE LEFT, FORMERLY AT NED'S POINT LIGHTHOUSE.

XXII

MONUMENT BEACH

GPS: (41.703225,-70.617634)

Directions from Previous Site: Follow Wings Neck Road back out to Barlows Landing Road. Take the 1st left onto Shore Road, follow it 0.8 miles, and turn left onto Valley Bars Circle. The next destination is straight ahead. (Distance: 3.5 mi. Driving Time: 10 mins.)

1. Little Bay Conservation Area

Located in the small village of Monument Beach, Little Bay Conservation Area is also known as Monk's Park. The parking area is bisected by railroad tracks that pass over the dirt road. From these tracks one gets a panoramic view of tree-covered peninsulas to the left and right. It is also an amazing place to watch the sun set, as it drops perfectly between the peninsulas.

The peninsula to the left is larger and has a bench and picnic table to enable you to enjoy views of Buzzards Bay and a few small islands that make up some of Monument Beach. From the tip of this peninsula, the Railroad Bridge is clearly visible to the northeast and the photo opportunities are endless.

The village of Monument Beach got its name from the Algonquin word "manomet." It became a popular summer resort in 1881, after a railroad line opened nearby that linked this area to New York, New Haven, and Hartford.

Important Info:
- Free parking
- No lifeguard
- No concessions

LITTLE BAY
CONSERVATION
AREA

THE RAILROAD BRIDGE
SEEN FROM THE LITTLE BAY
CONSERVATION AREA

SUNSET AT THE LITTLE
BAY CONSERVATION
AREA

Little Bay Conservation Area
Monument Beach

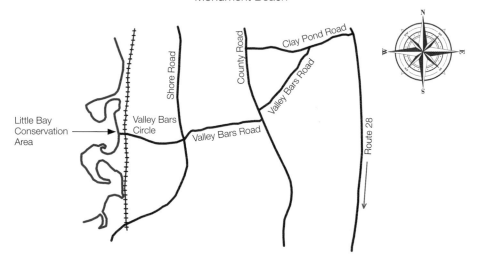

Shore Road

County Road

Clay Pond Road

Valley Bars Road

Little Bay
Conservation
Area

Valley Bars
Circle

Valley Bars Road

Route 28

N

W E

S

BOURNE

GPS: (41.71805,-70.63402)

Directions from Previous Site: Head back out to Shore Road; turn left, and follow it 2.2 miles. Turn left onto Monument Neck Road, take a slight right onto Presidents Road, and follow it 0.3 miles. Bear left onto Mashnee Road; follow it 1.5 miles to the next destination. (Distance: 4.5 mi. Driving Time: 12 mins.)

1. Mashnee Island

Possibly the least known island on Cape Cod, Mashnee Island is not really an island at all, as it is connected by an access road. There are signs for the "island" at the Bourne Rotary, near the bridge, but many people miss them as they head on and off the Cape on the highway. If you follow the signs, you will be led down Mashnee Road, which leads over a sandy spit out to the island itself. There are no places to park on the access road, so one must drive all the way out before seeing the unique community.

Unfortunately, it is basically a residential community with nowhere to park. Visitors to the beaches are generally dropped off, then picked up later.

From the beaches one can see the smoky-gray Railroad Bridge standing tall behind the tree line, only a little over a mile away. There is also a clear view of the wind turbine at the Massachusetts Maritime Academy, across the Cape Cod Canal. A walk on the beach at Mashnee Island is a beautiful and unexpected experience. Many visitors do not even know this little finger of land stretching out into Buzzards Bay exists, and it is not an easy place to visit because of the lack of parking or conveniences. The view, however, is worth the effort.

THE VIEW FROM MASHNEE ISLAND

BOURNE   145

Mashnee Island
Buzzards Bay

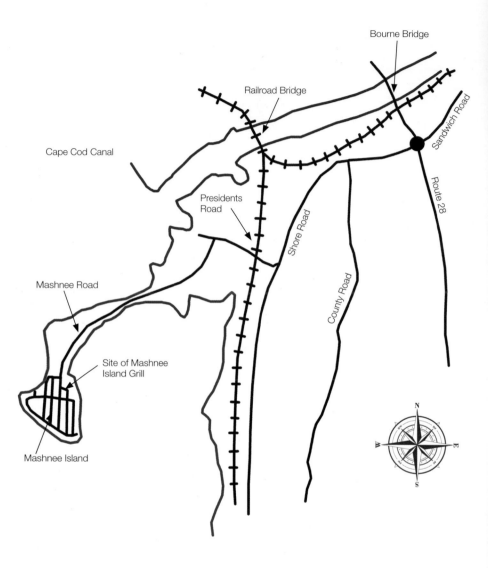

Bourne Bridge

Railroad Bridge

Sandwich Road

Cape Cod Canal

Route 28

Presidents Road

Shore Road

County Road

Mashnee Road

Site of Mashnee Island Grill

Mashnee Island

N

E

W

S

GPS: (41.740742,-70.613235)
Directions from Previous Site: Follow Mashnee Island Road back out onto Presidents Road. Stay on Presidents for 0.4 miles, then take a slight left onto Monument Neck Road. Continue onto Shore Road, follow it 0.2 miles, and turn left onto Bell Road. Follow it 0.3 miles to the parking area for the next destination. (Distance: 2.6 mi. Driving Time: 8 mins.)

2. Railroad Bridge

The third bridge along the Cape Cod Canal, the Railroad Bridge is a sight to behold. Easy to find by following Shore Road to Bell Road, this bridge is at the end of the paved Canal biking and walking path. There are two parking lots near the bridge: a small one almost directly under it and a larger one across the water from the Massachusetts Maritime Academy. This parking lot is at the mouth of the Canal and there are always flocks of birds trying to feed on fish caught in the rapidly moving tides.

The railroad bridge, crossing the Canal near Buzzards Bay, was the largest vertical lift bridge in history when it was built in 1935. When raised, it has a clearance of 135 feet. Seeing it in action is not easy, however, since train traffic is not as frequent as it used to be. The main stretch of the bridge sits high above the water, unless a train is approaching. However, there is always a chance of seeing a boat or several boats passing by. Whether tiny sailboats or gigantic barges, there is always traffic on the Canal.

Important Info:
• Free parking

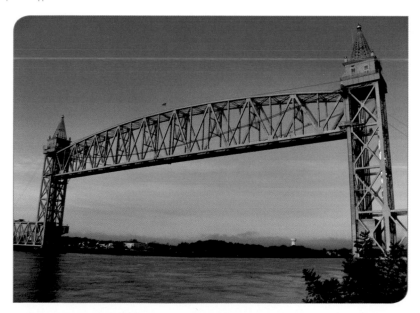

THE RAILROAD BRIDGE ACROSS THE CAPE COD CANAL.

THE RAILROAD BRIDGE ACROSS THE CAPE COD CANAL.

A SHIP PASSING BY THE RAILROAD BRIDGE.

GPS: (41.742415,-70.60535)

Directions from Previous Site: Follow Bell Road south, then take the 1st left onto Old Monument Neck Road. Follow it 0.4 miles, turn left onto Aptucxet Road. Turn left for the next destination which will be straight ahead. (Distance: .7 miles Driving Time: 3 mins.)

3. Aptucxet Trading Post & Gray Gables

The Windmill Gift Shop ushers you on a trip back nearly 400 years. Built in 1627, this was the first trading post used by the fledgling Plymouth Colony. The building that stands is a replica of the original, but the museum houses excavated pieces of the original building. A replica salt works is located on the grounds as well, consisting of two wooden buildings used to evaporate water from the salt using the sun.

The windmill at the entrance to the trading post was formerly on the grounds of 19th century actor Joseph Jefferson, friend and fishing companion of President Grover Cleveland. The Gray Gables railroad station sits less than a hundred feet from the Aptucxet Trading Post museum. It was created for President Grover Cleveland, whose summer home in Bourne was named Gray Gables. Beginning in 1892, it was the first Cape Cod summer White House.

The station is the original, not a replica, and has a regal flair to it, with its golden color fit for a president. The building was moved to the Aptucxet grounds in 1976. With the Canal in sight, this is a nice, shady spot to enjoy.

Important Info:
• Free parking
• Museum entrance fees: adults, $4; children $2.
• Open Memorial Day to Columbus Day

THE WINDMILL AT THE ENTRANCE TO THE APTUCXET TRADING POST.

APTUCXET TRADING POST

THE SALT WORKS AT THE APTUCXET TRADING POST.

THE APTUCXET TRADING POST WITH GRAY GABLES IN THE BACKGROUND.

GRAY GABLES STATION

4. Briggs-McDermott House

George Briggs had a key influence in Bourne's separation from Sandwich in 1884. He became one of the town's first selectmen and was a friend of Grover Cleveland. After his death, his 200-year-old house passed to Mercy Briggs McDermott and her husband, William.

Another historically significant building on the grounds is the Alonzo Booth Blacksmith Shop, built in 1888. It is the place where President Cleveland brought his horses to be shod. The shop was moved from the east side of Shore Road and restored in 1998. It is now is a fully working shop, with people operating the forge every day it is open.

The Briggs-McDermott House serves as the headquarters of Bourne's Society for Historical Preservation.

Important Info:
• Free parking at Bourne Library across the street at the Jonathan Bourne Library
• Open for tours from Memorial Day through Columbus Day, Tuesday through Saturday, from 11am to 3pm.

BRIGGS-MCDERMOTT HOUSE

ALONZO BOOTH BLACKSMITH SHOP

GPS: (41.746614,-70.588372)

Directions from Previous Site: Follow Sandwich Road east 0.7 miles; take 1st left after going underneath the Bourne Bridge. Follow it to the next destination. (Distance: .7 mi. Driving Time: 2 mins.)

5. Bourne Recreation Area

The Bourne Recreation Area can be hard to find despite the thousands of people who pass directly over it every day. The connector road that runs between the Bourne and Sagamore Bridges is the key. As you approach the Bourne Bridge, stay on Sandwich Road and go under the bridge. Just on the other side, a road goes to the left, toward the canal. There is parking on the right.

Picnic tables, where people can eat or just relax, are in the shadow of the massive steel bridge. You can walk along the Canal while listening to the rush of highway traffic passing overhead. It is a soothing sort of hum mixed with the gentle lapping of waves on the rocks.

Active railroad tracks pass along the Canal and should be carefully watched in case trains come along. The bike path can be used for walking, and on warmer days it is a busy place, with high numbers of bicyclists, runners, and skaters. The bike path is also an access road for government vehicles, but no other motorized traffic. It runs the entire seven- to eight-mile length of the Canal. This lesser-known area has a perfect mix of highway bustle and quiet solitude that should be experienced by any visitor to Cape Cod.

Important Info:
• Free Parking

BOURNE BRIDGE AT THE BOURNE RECREATION AREA

BOURNE RECREATION AREA

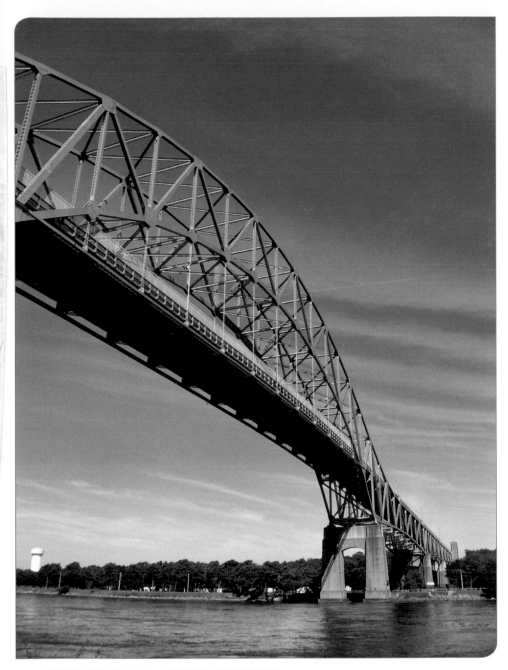

BOURNE BRIDGE AT THE BOURNE RECREATION AREA

Directions from Previous Site: Head back out to Sandwich Road, follow it 0.2 miles. Take a sharp right onto Rt. 6A. Follow it 0.2 miles; take the 1st exit at the rotary for the Bourne Bridge. I hope you enjoyed your trip around Cape Cod. Please, come back anytime!

LEAVING THE CAPE

THE BOURNE BRIDGE FROM BEHIND THE APTUCXET TRADING POST.

BIBLIOGRAPHY

Albright, E.J. "The Tony Costa Cape Cod Murders." *Cape Cod Today :: Cape Cod News and Information*. 11 Sept. 2007. Web: http://www.capecodtoday.com/blogs/index.php/2007/09/11/the_tony_costa_cape_cod_murders?blog=149. Sept.-Oct. 2011.

Cape Cod Highland Lighthouse Museum Attraction National Seashore Truro. 2010. Web: http://www.capecodlight.org/ Sept.-Oct. 2011.

Daniels, Clarece B. "Billingsgate Island." *Cape Cod History and Literature*. July 2006. Web: http://capecodhistory.us/Wellfleet-records/BillingsgateIsland.htm. Sept.-Oct. 2011.

1856 Country Store. Web: http://www.1856countrystore.com/. Sept.-Oct. 2011.

Falmouth Historical Society—Falmouth Museums on the Green. 2009. Web: http://www.falmouthhistoricalsociety.org/. Sept.-Oct. 2011.

Green, E. *Names of the Land.* Connecticut: The Globe Pequot Press, 1982.

Hallet's Store. Web. Sept.-Oct. 2011. Web: http://www.hallets.com/.

Heritage Museums and Gardens Celebrating the American Spirit. Web: http://www.heritagemuseumsandgardens.org/. Sept.-Oct. 2011.

The Historical Society of Old Yarmouth. Web:http://www.hsoy.org. Sept.-Oct. 2011.

"Marconi's Wellfleet (Cape Cod) Wireless - Stormfax®." *Marconi's Wellfleet Wireless - Stormfax*. 2003. Web: http://www.stormfax.com/wireless.htm Sept.-Oct. 2011.

New England Lighthouses: A Virtual Guide —Photos,history, Tours, Cruises, Coastal Accommodations and More. Web: http://lighthouse.cc/. Sept.-Oct. 2011.

"Old Bourne Village, Bourne Historical Society, Bourne, Cape Cod, MA." *Bourne Historical Society, Bourne, Cape Cod, MA*. 2008. Web: http://www.bournehistoricalsociety.org/.bournevillage.html Sept.-Oct. 2011.

Pilgrim Monument and Museum - Home. 2009. Web: http://pilgrim-monument.org/ Sept.-Oct. 2011.

"Pursuing the Paranormal: "In His Garden"" *Cape Cod Today :: Cape Cod News and Information*. 13 Sept. 2007. Web: http://www.capecodtoday.com/blogs/index.php/2007/09/13/pursuing_the_paranormal_5?blog=130. Sept.-Oct. 2011.

Race Point Light Station. Web: http://web.me.com/jenkinsgroup/Race_Point/Welcome.html. Sept.-Oct. 2011.

"Sandy Neck Beach." *Cape Cod Recreation—Cape Cod Premier Recreation and Fitness Directory - For Fun - For Fitness - For Your Next Vacation*. 2001. Web: http://www.capecodrec.com/4wheeling/sandyneck/ Sept.-Oct. 2011.

"USA Oldest Wooden Jail." *Cape And Islands Paranormal Research Society & Cape Cod's Haunted & History Tours*. Web: http://www.caiprs.com/Theoldjail.htm Sept.-Oct. 2011.

INDEX

ACKNOWLEDGMENTS

I could not have completed this book without the love and support of so many people. Thanks to my family, Mom, Dad, Serpa, Kate, Matt, Lindsay, Ashley, my Aunts Susie, Kelly, and Emma; my Uncles Eric, Bob, Steve, and John; my cousins, nieces, and nephews, Nina and Grampa, and my Nana. Thanks also to my friends Meg, Barry, John, Deanna, Steve, and Emily, to my Marsh family and everyone else. A part of each of you is in this book! I have been truly blessed.

SUNSET AT BOUND BROOK ISLAND